Michael Jones

RESET

"*Reset* is a witty and insightful book written by CFO and former mortgage loan originator, Michael Jones. It's a humorous yet realistic look into the fast-paced world of mortgage lending, and it was awesome to see how Michael used *Miracle Morning* to revive and jump-start a young, but frustrated LO's career.

"On the brink of burnout, frustrated at his lack of self-discipline and quickly-dwindling book of business, the main character's personal life was starting to crumble, but by identifying the problems and implementing S.A.V.E.R.S., he was able to regain control of his life, improve his work habits and experience success!

"So . . . for all you struggling young professionals trying to juggle it all, this is a must read! I am also beyond excited to see my name in print—it never gets old, folks!"

— Hal Elrod
#1 Bestselling Author
The Miracle Morning
MiracleMorningBook.com

CONTENTS

CONTENTS
CONTINUED

ACKNOWLEDGMENTS

A big thank you to my loving wife who was willing to sacrifice afternoons and evenings to provide me with the quiet time necessary to write this book without feeling guilty.

I cannot thank my editor, Blake Atwood, enough for his work and contribution on this book. While I enjoy writing, I wouldn't call myself an excellent writer and certainly not an experienced one. Blake helped walk me through the process from start to finish. At one point, this book was only ten chapters with twenty pages in each chapter! If you're looking for an editor and you're not sure where to start, I recommend reaching out to Blake and checking out his book on the subject, *Don't Fear the Reaper: Why Every Author Needs an Editor*.

Another big thank you to my father, Roy, for providing me encouragement to pursue the idea of writing a book. Without his support, *Reset* would still be rolling around in the back of my head as a long-time regret for never being written. He is without a doubt my best sounding board.

A huge thank you to Donna Fisher who is a mortgage veteran, a member of the Georgetown Mortgage Executive team, and an excellent writer herself. Her contributions to Reset were invaluable and I look forward to working with her on future projects.

And finally, thank you to Brett Levy, an old mentor and friend who took the time to read through the novel with only a limited understanding of the industry.

CHAPTER 1
WELCOME TO THE RAT RACE

Mark rubbed his eyes as he took a moment to clear his thoughts. A quick glance at the bottom of his computer screen confirmed what his body felt: it was mid-afternoon, around 3:00 p.m.

The grind was on.

He couldn't complain though. It was busy season in the residential mortgage business and business was good. He knew that over the next few months he'd make the majority of his income for the year. Then he'd be able to relax a little bit when the winter slow time hit around November. It was a cyclical business to be certain, and loan officers who forgot that were in for lean times when it wasn't peak season.

He glanced at the right side of his desk and felt his face drop. *Almost forgot about those.* There were four recent mortgage application files to go through and each file would take the better part of an hour to thoroughly review, organize, scan, and upload into his loan origination software or LOS. To make matters worse, he hadn't sourced these files. Another loan officer in the office had quit and Mark had inherited these files because his production was down.

Mark turned away from the papers, choosing instead to read a recent email—until the chirp of his cell phone interrupted him. He glanced at the number but didn't recognize the caller. Yet an unrecognized number in the mortgage business wasn't a bad thing. Almost imperceptibly, his pulse quickened at the thought of a new client. After all these years, Mark still enjoyed the thrill of the hunt. Pulling up a blank Word document, Mark took the call.

"Hello, this is Mortgage Mark. How may I be of service?"

Mark always answered the phone and made introductions with this silly tag line. As goofy as it seemed, he was regularly recognized as Mortgage Mark, which was great because it allowed him to always be softly selling.

He didn't recognize the caller's voice on the other end.

"Hi Mark, this is Janet Keller. I'm friends with Denise Jones. You recently helped her get a mortgage for her home and I'm looking to get pre-qualified. She said she'd had a good experience with you."

"Hi Janet, thank you for reaching out to me! I greatly appreciate Denise spreading the word about her experience. She was wonderful to work with. Let me start with a few questions to make sure we're on the right track. Does that sound good?"

"Absolutely. Fire away!"

"Great! This won't take long, but it will save us a lot of time in the long run." It had taken him the better part of a year to perfect his opening dialogue, but he attributed some of his success to having in-depth discussions with prospects up front.

"First, have you ever been through the home-buying process?"

"No, I haven't actually. I was a little confused where to start, which is what prompted the conversation with Denise. We actually work together and I followed her purchase from start to finish during our morning coffee. It seems very complicated."

"Well, that's great to hear you're looking at your first home. You know, it's gotten a bit tougher over the last few years, primarily from a documentation standpoint. Nowadays, loans have to be fully documented with no room for doubt about how income is earned, where the down payment will come from, and what the home will be used for. In the grand scheme of things, this is very good for the homeowner and for the economy as a whole, but when you're in the middle of qualifying for a loan, it can make you want to pull your hair out. My goal is to make this as smooth as possible for you so that you have a wonderful home-buying experience you'll rave about."

"Okay, that sounds great. What's next?"

"Since this is your first home, let's start with the basic loan programs and go from there." Mark then launched into an hour-long dialogue with his prospect, discussing various loan programs and their advantages and what Janet needed in order to qualify for a home loan. By the end of the call, he felt he'd attained a very good understanding of his prospect. In fact, he'd even received a commitment from her that she'd get him everything he needed within the next few days.

"Janet, it was an absolute pleasure speaking with you, and I'll reach out to you first thing next week to see if you've been able to gather everything we need. Please don't hesitate to call me any time with questions or concerns."

Mark hung up at exactly 4:15 p.m. He stared intently through his window with the foreboding sense that he was missing something. He checked his Outlook calendar and scanned for any pending appointments. There was nothing on the schedule, but he noticed how strange it was to be free this early in the day.

Something nagged at him as he mindlessly checked his Facebook and searched for any leads on social media. Thirty minutes of pointless scrolling later, it hit him: *Jason's soccer game*! He grabbed his phone and pulled up the last text conversation with his wife, a growing pit of despair forming in his stomach. A few screen slides down, his fears were confirmed: his son had a game scheduled at 5:00 and it was easily a thirty minute drive from his office to the fields.

Frantic, Mark slammed his laptop shut, threw the computer in his bag, and ran to his car. Just as he exited the building, he slapped his forehead and muttered words he couldn't say at home. He ran back to his office, grabbed the library of files off his desk, and shoved them into his bag. Running down the hall of his office for a second time, Mark scolded himself as he passed by his colleagues' cubes. He hated looking flustered, but that had become almost synonymous with his famous tagline Mortgage Mark. He was known throughout the office for working hard, but he was also known for jumping from one meeting to the next and never being on top of his schedule.

After what felt like an eternity, Mark made it to his black Mercedes coupe and tossed his belongings in the back seat. With a quick glance at his watch, Mark settled into the driver's seat and punched the ignition. At this rate, he was likely going to miss nearly the entire first half of the game. He could see Jason scanning the sidelines to see if dad had missed yet another game.

The pit in his stomach deepened.

Cruising on the highway helped slightly, but Mark regularly used this time to catch up on phone calls. He looked at the number scribbled on his palm and called a prospect. Nearly halfway to the game, Mortgage Mark had already launched into another thorough prospect call that would surely last longer than the car ride.

Sure enough, as Mark pulled into an open parking spot at the soccer field and stepped out of the car, the prospect conversation was in full swing. It's not that he wouldn't interrupt the conversation, but he was always concerned about the impression it left with the prospect and whether that one impression would mean he'd lose them. Nothing was more important than his son's game, but this was his livelihood! This is how he could afford to give his son and family opportunities, right? And, if he was being perfectly honest, he had a sense of fulfillment from constantly being busy.

Why just work smart when you can work hard too?

He paced the sidelines for a few minutes, trying to make eye contact with his little boy on the field while wrapping up the conversation with his prospect. The ref blew the whistle for halftime. Mark interrupted his prospect.

"Stan, I really appreciate you taking the time to speak with me, and I'm sorry for interrupting you, but I just arrived at my son's soccer game, and I want to spend some time with him during halftime. Would it be okay if we continued this conversation later? Tomorrow morning? That's great, talk to you then."

Mark exchanged a knowing glance with his wife, Jennifer, feeling the daggers being plunged into his conscience as he quickly shuffled his way through a sea of little boys to reach his son. Jason was only five and looked adorable in his soccer cleats and jersey. Mark liked to think of himself as a man's man but his kid was a rare soft spot in his heart.

"Hey son! You looked great out there! How are you doing?"

Jason looked up at his dad with a slightly disappointed look. "It's okay, dad. You missed a lot of the half. I helped score a goal!"

This cut Mark deeply. He knew how important soccer was to his son and how rarely this sort of thing happened. And he'd missed it!

"That's awesome, buddy! I'm so sorry I was late! But I'm here now, and I can't wait to watch you."

Jason tried to smile but Mark saw the all-too familiar tremble in his bottom lip, still obviously upset that his dad had missed his big accomplishment.

I feel like such a heel.

Just then, Jennifer slid up to Mark and hissed in his ear. "We talked about this all morning. How could you be late?"

Mark grabbed her hand and gave it a squeeze to let her know that he acknowledged the rebuke, but that he was not going to engage in an argument.

"It was a busy day at work, but I'm here now."

CHAPTER 2
WHERE'S THE RESET BUTTON?

Mark didn't have much of an appetite at dinner after the soccer game but now, as he lay in Jason's tiny bed gently stroking his head, his stomach began to growl. Mark reflected back on the day.

When did things go wrong?

That morning had started out better than expected. Mark left the house on time with breakfast in hand and had even made it to work slightly ahead of schedule. But throughout the morning, Mark had been derailed by a few unexpected calls and distractions that prevented him from making the progress he'd promised himself he'd make the day before. By the afternoon, his schedule was moot. He'd called an audible and did whatever was necessary to keep his team on the offensive.

Unfortunately, this had been Mortgage Mark's norm for nearly two years. As more people exited the mortgage business and as Mark had become more well-known around town, his days had become absolute blurs. It was all he could do to keep his head above water. Drowning in work, he was generally exhausted when he got home.

Brought back to reality when Jason coughed softly, Mark thought back to almost missing the soccer game. Afterwards, the family had gone to their son's favorite restaurant, Chuck-E-Cheese, to celebrate the victory and Jason's essential role in it. While their son played video games and ran through hundreds of feet of play equipment, Jennifer and Mark debriefed on the day.

"I don't understand why you continue to miss his games like this. We talked about it this morning."

"I know, I know. I don't know why I didn't put it in my calendar. I just let myself get too busy when I got to work."

"He doesn't care about that. He doesn't understand. All he sees is that dad didn't make it on time and that you don't care about what's important to him. It kills him."

"Geez, Jen, I get it. Don't you get that I hate missing important things like this, too? Being there for him is so important to me! It's just that I have to make sure I'm taking care of my clients so that I *can* be there for him."

Jennifer shook her head in disagreement and disbelief. "You keep saying how important it is to you, but you continue to fall short. How can that be? What you're doing and what you're saying are to-tally out of sync."

As Mark listened to Jason's peaceful breathing, he replayed that sentence over and over: "<u>What you're doing and what you're saying are totally out of sync.</u>"

What Jennifer was basically telling him was that he didn't have any integrity. He wasn't staying true to his word and following through on what he said he would. The pit formed in Mark's stom-ach again. He felt like he was trapped in quicksand that would never allow him to move past their constant arguments about his integrity.

Oddly enough, integrity was one of the most important pillars Mark clung to in his business. If he told his client that their interest rate would be a certain percentage, he would *always* honor that, even if it meant he would incur a loss on the transaction. He often liked to say that his word was stronger than oak.

Apparently that only applied to his business dealings.

Mark lifted himself from the bed and kissed Jason's head one last time. He walked down the hallway toward Jennifer's faint snores. *I'm not even sure she wants to be in the same bed with me right now.* As he turned into their doorway, he glimpsed through the open door of his office. Sitting right where he'd placed them when they'd all gotten home were those files. The files that were slowly killing him.

With one hand on the doorframe, he paused and let out a deep sigh. He'd either have to work longer tomorrow or forego planned prospect calls to catch up. The saga of frustration continued with no end in sight. He wanted to do better.

Where's the reset button?

All he wanted was to run a well-oiled origination machine and be able to relax with his family at home, feeling satisfied he'd done everything he could—but he just couldn't catch his breath. Mark silently got ready for the night and slipped into his side of the bed. Jennifer remained frozen and silent. She was either asleep, or more likely, seething. Mark decided his odds were better by letting things settle overnight. He turned onto his side away from Jennifer and tried to fall asleep.

CHAPTER 3
A MAN OF INTEGRITY

The next day passed the same as the last, save their weekly Friday meetings. David, the branch manager, was relatively well-respected, but most everyone felt the meetings were a waste of time. As one of the branch's average producers with years of experience, Mark felt that attending was a bit below him. On the rare occasion that he did attend, he'd sit in the back with his iPad and respond to client messages, or pass the time by making changes to his fantasy football team on ESPN. Mark was always a team player, but felt little need to be plugged in.

He only attended today because he'd heard there would be important program changes. And he was glad he did: he was mentioned quite frequently in the branch's rankings. While he had been #8 out of their fifteen producers last month, his efficiency rating had put him in the lower 80th percentile, which meant that he had to work significantly harder—along with the processors and underwriters his company used—to close his files relative to the rest of the branch.

Reflecting back on the last month, his files hadn't been a complete train wreck, but he had checked out a bit as he'd been focused on making more prospect calls. He'd also been focused on something much more personal, which he hadn't mentioned to anyone—not even his best friend Caleb. Mark and his wife had been trying to conceive their second child. Clearly, those dual focuses had hit his numbers. This trend couldn't continue if he wanted to improve his production.

David regularly talked about how branch resources would be focused on the files that were best positioned to close and fund. If Mark continued to submit train wreck files, he might get blackballed by processors and underwriters. He'd heard of this happening at other companies. Supposedly, a processor or underwriter gets so fed up with your work, they take easier files ahead of yours, or worse yet, they stop granting exceptions, which makes the loan officer's job much more difficult. Many times the originator would even have to switch companies because the lack of support turned into a death spiral. The LO's files wouldn't get the same attention as the others and ultimately the originator's reputation suffered.

After the meeting, Mark briefly met with David to acknowledge that he'd work on his efficiency numbers. Mark then dashed to his office to take care of the files he'd neglected the night before. As his LOS loaded for the day, Mark looked at his calendar to see a networking meeting scheduled for 4:30 p.m. at a restaurant a few blocks away. He regretted making the appointment now with all he had on his plate, however this meeting was part of his sales strategy. Given his recent track record, he needed to make this event.

As Mark began reviewing his first file, integrity was top of mind. He had always prided himself on being a man of his word—in fact, his follow through is what had made him successful in this business in the first place. Over the years, he'd won the business of countless customers and referral partners because he had simply returned a call when he said he would. But now, as his personal and professional lives were getting busier, he was allowing himself to slip.

Mark finished his review a little before noon, satisfied that he'd checked all the important information to merit a good underwriting decision. He stretched in his chair and felt his stomach grumble—lunch time! Making his way to the office kitchen, he was growing less excited about the lunch he'd packed for himself.

A few months back, he and Jennifer had met with their financial advisor. It had become very clear that they were spending way too much money on eating out. Had they been saving what they were spending on food, they would have been able to send Jason to college by the time he was twelve. After that staggering realization, they'd created a grocery and meal plan to better manage their finances. Mark was struggling to stick to it.

The Black Forest ham and cheddar cheese sandwich with plenty of mayonnaise and mustard had seemed so appetizing a few hours ago! He'd been impressed with himself for throwing in an apple and a bag of cashews to round out a healthy and cheap lunch. But that was early morning, higher energy Mark. Midday and low energy Mark was craving the Chipotle at the bottom floor of their retail office location.

It's relatively healthy and if I don't get a drink, it'll only be a few bucks. I can put it on my personal credit card and pay it off so that it won't hit the main checking account.

Mark felt a little guilty about clearly trying to be deceptive, but doggonnit, he worked hard and deserved this. He shut the door to the fridge and walked defiantly toward the exit.

Much later, with burrito grease still rumbling in his stomach with his wife lying beside him in bed, Mark would realize he'd taken yet another step in losing his integrity.

The rest of the afternoon went off without a hitch for the most part. Mark was faithful in making his calls and made a few final checks for his closing on Monday. It wasn't always guaranteed, but he'd had an incredibly good track record with closing on time. That didn't mean it always happened gracefully. In fact, if he were to sit down and do the math—which he didn't have time for—he would have discovered that roughly 60 percent of his closings were what he called "hair-on-fire" closings. In other words, a clear-to-close was provided about 72 hours prior to closing, and then it became a mad dash with the doc prep attorneys and title company to prepare a Closing Disclosure, send it to the client for review, and hit the closing table. It was maddening to him to never seem to get ahead of the curve. Something always popped up.

————

Mark slumped in his chair and glanced at his computer clock: 3:15 on a Friday afternoon. His legs bounced. There was probably enough time to make a few quick client calls or check in with his referral partners, but he really just didn't feel like it. He reviewed his pipeline but everything appeared to be in order. Mark knew that being idle was a complete waste of his time and that time was money, but he just couldn't bring himself to be fully productive in this final hour or so before happy hour.

Opening up his browser, Mark clicked on Favorites and logged on to Facebook. After a few minutes, he'd scrolled past the most recent updates: his sister and her new puppy frolicking in the grass, a few college friends with their families, and so on. He switched over to CNBC. Surprise, surprise. The economy wasn't doing as well as expected and analysts were speculating about delays by the Fed in raising interest rates. Other articles discussed property bubbles looming over the horizon. More gloom and doom. It could be monotonous to sift through all of the economic news out there, each analyst disagreeing with the next, but by and large this controlled interest rates, which controlled what happened to his borrowers, which controlled his business.

Tiring of the dire economic outlook, Mark sighed as he logged on to LinkedIn. Of all the sites he frequented, LinkedIn appeared to be the most helpful. Not only did this alert him to friends and acquaintances changing jobs and getting promotions, but he could also see who was connecting to whom. Thinking tactically over the years, Mark had connected with several individuals he'd deemed to be competitors so that he could track their connections with realtors, corporate executives, and other industry professionals. If he noticed a movement in someone's network, he'd analyze what that meant to him and whether he should be doing something about it.

Today, he noticed that several of his competitors had begun following Todd Duncan. Mark spoke the name aloud, trying to locate in his mind who that was. As he slowly stroked his week-old beard and stared at Todd Duncan's picture, the reference emerged from the fog. Mark vaguely remembered reading about Todd when he had first gotten into mortgage lending. In fact, his old (and slightly forgotten) friend and colleague, Tyler, had been pretty big on Todd Duncan when Mark first got into the industry.

For one reason or another, Mark just couldn't bring himself to pay attention to people like Todd Duncan. He felt that what they did to earn business was feel-good nonsense that amounted to nothing at the end of the day. Affirmations, meditation, rituals, and visualizations all seemed like a joke. The leaders of these movements were probably milking poor saps that were simply looking for direction in life. Mark had done just fine without leadership from these motivational speakers.

But as Mark thought a bit longer, he remembered that Tyler had seemed to gain ground faster than he had. Whether it was setting up realtor meetings or successfully closing a loan for a client, the work had seemed to come a little faster for Tyler than it had for Mark. Mark thought about this for a few moments before clicking on Todd Duncan's LinkedIn profile. As the profile was loaded, his computer chimed and a big reminder popped up, obscuring most of the screen. It was 4:00 and time to head to the networking meeting.

Intending to look at Todd's profile later, Mark put his computer to sleep and grabbed his belongings. Stepping outside his office to the main cubicle area, Mark surveyed the office floor. Even for a Friday, the office looked fairly empty. *Makes sense. The weather's beautiful and it's the first of the month.* The office was busiest at the end of the month when the bulk of the loan officer's loans closed.

Walking to the exit, Mark said his goodbyes and stopped by the fridge to throw out his lunch that had gone uneaten—again.

Shame on you, Mark. But that's okay. You'll make it up later, right?

CHAPTER 4
FEEL-GOODERY NONSENSE

An hour into Happy Hour and Mark was growing impatient that he had yet to make any meaningful contacts. He reflected for a moment on his first networking events a decade before. Back then, networking was a service professional's best kept secret. It hadn't become trendy yet, and finding events was difficult as most people were still trying to figure out how to use the Internet for things besides news and e-mail.

He remembered how he'd eagerly thrown himself into conversations and made every attempt to truly connect with someone. He had to—it was how he'd put food on the table. You never knew when the person you were speaking with would want to buy or refinance. And even if the immediate person didn't need a home loan, surely they would know someone who would! In those days, networking was like shooting fish in a barrel. Throw the high-flying days of the mortgage business into the mix and Mortgage Mark had been living large.

But not now.

Numerous sites with the sole purpose of networking brought individuals from all walks of life together—for better or worse. There were always the financial advisors, dressed in their suits and ties, floating from conversation to conversation in search of someone they felt had enough money worth talking to.

Then you had the multi-level marketers. Oh, the MLMs. Mark almost admired their tenacity. *Almost.* Typically, they were selling products they didn't fully understand to an unknowing consumer who understood even less. And it was always health-related! How could you go wrong? Everyone was either too fat or too lazy to be in shape so they'd rely on potions and powders contained in brightly colored packaging to feel better about themselves.

To round out the mix, there were always about four insurance agents for every twenty people. God help 'em. In the real estate totem pole, these folks found themselves squarely at the bottom. Banks required insurance, so insurance agents were needed, but largely as an afterthought. They always competed on price. It was a necessary evil but all your average borrower cared about the bottom line monthly payment, not necessarily the coverage they needed or wanted. Insurance agents had to amass hundreds of clients before they could consider themselves stable. Even then, they were subject to what pricing the carriers offered. Mark had learned how to identify an agent and how to steer clear.

Much to his chagrin, the realtors in the room probably felt the same way about *him.* Realtors sat atop the real estate totem pole. Most buyers talked to a realtor before they ever dreamed of speaking with a mortgage banker. Who could blame them? These days, qualifying for a loan was a tedious process that drained all joy from buying a home.

Back in the present, Mark considered this particular networking event a bust. He hadn't run into a single realtor, and most of the folks he did speak with weren't remotely interested in purchasing a home or refinancing. The refi business had dried up a bit with recent increases in interest rates.

It wasn't as bad as 2013 though. Lord help us. The markets had changed so quickly and unexpectedly that some small independent mortgage banks and brokers had gone out of business. With the ease of refinance business, they had forsaken their lifeline, the realtor. Mark had a few rough months as he was caught flat-footed. Luckily, he had always maintained a steady stream of communication with his agents, but he'd learned a valuable lesson to not let his refinance business consume more than 50 to 60 percent of his pipeline and his time. *Things have certainly chan . . .*

"Mark?"

Mark gazed at the man in front of him. He'd been so engrossed in bashing his fellow networkers that he'd momentarily forgotten what was going on around him. Somehow this person knew his name. He focused toward the sound of the voice and was shocked to see his old colleague Tyler working his way through the crowd.

"Hey, Tyler, how's it going?" Mark exclaimed with a smile on his face. The men grasped hands and Mark motioned for Tyler to take a seat next to him. It had been a long time since they'd seen each other and Mark was genuinely happy to see his old friend. Dallas was growing like crazy and while Mark had chosen to move to the suburbs, Tyler had stayed in the city. *Wow. Tyler looks in great shape.*

Mark grew self-conscious as he took inventory of himself. At forty, he wasn't in terrible shape, but the pooch around his stomach wasn't doing him any favors plus he didn't feel as energetic as he used to. A combination of poor eating (but delicious burritos) and zero physical activity had taken its toll over the last few years. Jennifer had tried relentlessly to get him to be healthier but the drive just wasn't there.

Tyler, on the other hand, looked like he stayed active and was ready to conquer the world. Mark wondered if he still stuck to his morning routines. Back when they'd first started working together, Tyler would show up with a bag full of workout clothes, vitamins, and protein shakes. Mark would often call him a meathead and take jabs at him. Now he wished he'd had that kind of discipline.

"I'm doing great," Tyler responded as he took the seat next to Mark. "You look like you're doing well too. It's been awhile, hasn't it?"

"Yeah, it has. Where are you at nowadays? Last time we saw each other you were with NorthTexas Funding."

Mark was curious to hear Tyler's answer. Loan officers were notorious for jumping around from company to company. Typically, successful loan officers stuck with a company because the pain of learning another mortgage company's operations was too great. You never knew what you were getting into. It could be a disaster. Mark had made this mistake once after he'd been in the business for a year or two. The sirens of higher pay and more products had lured him into the rocks of origination disaster. The shop he had jumped ship for had terrible processes and even worse employee morale. After a few months Mark cut his losses and crawled back to his previous employer. Thankfully, they'd taken him back.

"I'm actually with HomeSource Mortgage and I'm a branch manager. I joined them, oh," Tyler trailed off as he searched for the date. "I guess it's been about two years now. Man, time really flies. It's honestly been great. I wasn't totally unhappy at NorthTexas Funding, but there were some management changes and it just completely lost its culture. I had a few connections at HomeSource Mortgage who seemed very happy with the direction that their company was taking. After doing some digging, I found that I really clicked with their culture. They believe in empowering their people and they have the right mindsets. I couldn't be happier."

Mark smiled and nodded. *That's what they all say.* He was used to hearing this sort of response. All loan officers—and realtors for that matter—made their companies sound like the best places in the world to work. It was probably an insecurity thing. That person didn't want to look like a chump for sticking with a place that sucked.

He wasn't familiar with HomeSource Mortgage though. Maybe he'd heard them in passing or had seen an event they'd sponsored.

"So no road bumps or issues?" Mark asked, digging a little further for the full story.

"Oh, don't get me wrong. The learning curve after joining any company is always a little tough, and there's always things that change that require everyone to sync up, but by and large it's been smooth. Since starting my branch, I've gotten lots of support from the Executive Management Team who places a big emphasis on staying connected to the Branch Managers and supporting their business model. We have regular calls with our Regional Managers and I've even been invited to sit on their Leadership Council where I get to weigh in on issues that will impact myself and my team. The home office conducts lots of fun contests and really makes their employees feel like family. I even get surprises from them for holidays, birthdays, and branch recognitions. It's just got a really great feel."

"Wow, branch manager now. You've really moved up in the world!" *Is he working himself silly like I am?*

"Hah, thanks. It's really not that tough if you build a good team. We have a strict hiring policy to make sure we work well as a team. I've got two other loan officers under me, as well as a branch processor and a loan officer assistant. It took a while to piece the team together, but it's been very good. We keep each other accountable and really sharpen each other."

"Man, that's great." *For you.*

Things seemed to be going genuinely well for Tyler which made Mark feel bad about the herky-jerky nature of his own business and success.

Mark leaned in closer. "Hey, I came across Todd Duncan's profile on LinkedIn today. Do you still follow Todd's material?"

"I sure do, buddy. Hands down, Todd's systems are the primary contributor to my success. Thankfully, HomeSource Mortgage fully embraces and promotes the program and techniques that keep me motivated and accountable. That was one thing missing from North Texas Funding and was critical to me joining HomeSource. In fact, it was Todd's Sales Mastery conference two years ago that really changed the way I do business. Actually, it changed the way I do a lot of things."

Mark's eyes widened. *You've got to be kidding me.* Tyler continued.

"There was a guest speaker at the conference by the name of Hal Elrod. If you haven't heard of him, his story is incredible. The guy literally died, was revived and made a full recovery from a horrific accident. There was a head-on collision on the highway, and you can guess how that went. Numerous broken bones, months of recovery, you get the gist. A few years later after making a relatively full recovery, he got creamed in the financial crisis. He says that's when he truly hit rock bottom. To him, dying and recovering was way easier. On the verge of losing his home, his business, and his way, he developed what he calls The Miracle Morning. It's a . . ."

"Wait a second. Is this guy in the mortgage business?" *Where's he going with this story?*

"No, actually. Todd Duncan was so interested in his story, he brought Hal in to give us a fresh perspective. There's been a few of what I would call game-changers in my life, and this was one of those moments. So back to what a Miracle Morning is."

As Tyler launched back into Hal Elrod and his Miracle Morning, Mark's interest waned. He was genuinely happy for Tyler that he had found something he was passionate about, but Tyler had always been that way. He quickly jumped on to a fad or feel-goodery thinking and then proceeded to preach that gospel to anyone he spoke with. Mark nodded politely and took another sip of his beer as Tyler discussed the six parts of a Miracle Morning. As he suspected, three of the six steps involved visualizations, affirmations, and meditation, a.k.a. delusional thinking. Tyler's final discussion point about the Miracle Morning made Mark snort beer out of his nose.

"You get up at what time?"

"I've been doing it for a while now, but I get up at 4:45 a.m. every single morning," Tyler calmly responded. He'd probably given that response a hundred times by now.

Mark was still shocked. *Who woke up that early unless they had to travel?* As he washed the beer off his tie, he pressed further. "What about the weekends?"

"Especially the weekends."

Am I allowed to throw a beer at a friend?

Sensing that Mark was having a hard time wrapping his mind around this new way of life, Tyler switched to a different topic. For the rest of the networking event, the two discussed their wives, marriage, fatherhood, and the "good ol' days." It was surprising how similar their lives were even though they hadn't kept in touch. They'd married about the same time and even had kids around the same age.

Sensing an opening in the discussion, Mark asked what he'd been dying to the whole time.

"So Tyler, I've been curious to ask this whole time, and I can't part ways without asking." He grinned sheepishly before blurting. "How's your production this year?"

Production numbers were the benchmark for any sales professional. Mark was hoping to hear that Tyler had likewise been stuck around five to seven units per month. The mortgage business had been tough the last few years. In this market, even Mark's numbers were considered fairly successful.

Tyler smiled and said, "I'm doing about thirty units per month for seven million dollars in personal production. My team's at about fifty units total for just shy of ten million a month."

Mark felt the oxygen sucked from lungs like being hit in the stomach. He nonchalantly blinked a few times, trying not to show that he was at a complete loss. *Thirty units of personal production?*

Mark had heard similar stories over the years, but those loan officers always seemed to be on the edge of legend. You'd hear about them but never come into contact with them, and that was in the high-flying days when *anyone* could get a loan and just about *any* loan could get approved. To have thirty units of personal production in this lending and regulatory environment was incredible.

If Mark felt bad before, it was nothing compared to this new knot in his stomach. He knew it was ridiculous to feel this way, but he was a competitive person and had always thought of himself as a better originator than Tyler. He felt a pang of guilt for being jealous of his friend's good fortune. Not wanting to appear catty, he offered the most sincere congratulations he could.

"Wow, Tyler, that's really amazing. That's quite an accomplishment. I know you're a sharp guy and I don't want to belittle your success, but what do you attribute that level of success to?" Mark knew the answer before he heard it. It wasn't what he wanted to hear. He wanted a roadmap, a solution, a checklist—something he could easily pick up and recreate.

With a big smile and a sincere laugh, Tyler laid his hand on Mark's shoulder and exclaimed, "My Miracle Morning, of course!"

———

A few hours later, Mark was still mulling over the conversation. *Damn that feel-goodery talk.* He took a few deep breaths as he ran his hands through his hair. He'd learned this technique from a barber a few years ago. The head was a hotbed of pleasure and pain receptors. By stroking your head, you were giving your mind and body an opportunity to relax and reset.

Why was he feeling this way? He was angry at himself for feeling so foolish toward a friend. Sure, they hadn't spent much time together the past few years and had always had a friendly rivalry, but Mark felt it was nonsense for him to feel this way. Diving into his thoughts,

Mark finally realized why Tyler's success and methods bothered him.

Mark whispered the brutal truth into the darkness: "I'm not happy with where my life is at."

This admission made him feel both relieved and a little worried. He was able to let go of his ill feelings about the earlier conversation, but now he had to face that he simply wasn't doing as well as he wanted to be doing. His production was okay, but he was already falling behind the goals he'd set for himself—for his family, really.

He wanted to provide the lifestyle that he and Jennifer didn't get to enjoy when they were kids—to take trips whenever they wanted to, go to concerts and plays, put Jason into the best schools and athletic programs. Plus, they were trying to add to their family. Now his mind raced, trying to figure out where he had gone astray this year. These last *few* years, really.

Great. Now I'm worked up and won't be able to sleep. Mark silently and slowly lifted himself up from the bed, careful not to wake Jennifer. He hated when this happened to him. His only remedy was to go downstairs and mindlessly watch TV until he couldn't keep his eyes open. Then, he'd shut the house down and slip back into bed.

This week will be different, he assured himself as he flopped down onto the couch. As the TV warmed up and light filled the living room downstairs, Mark already felt a little better.

Next week is going to be great.

CHAPTER 5
WHEN IT RAINS, IT POURS

"I'm sorry. Will you please explain this escrow account to me one more time? I know you've gone over it several times, but it just isn't sticking."

It was Monday at the closing table with Ms. Adams, a kind woman in her mid-fifties. Today was the first time she'd ever purchased a home by herself. She'd been skittish through the whole process, and Mark thought it was no small miracle she was sitting at the table now. Unfortunately for Ms. Adams, her husband had died of a sudden heart attack at work. No warning, no chance. She was downsizing, and she'd relied heavily on Mark's guidance over the last few months.

In all honesty, this was one of Mark's favorite type of clients. A client who heavily relied on him for advice and truly trusted him was a client who wasn't going to leave him for an online competitor just because of a one-eighth difference in the rate or a few hundred dollars in fees. They took more time, but an ace in the hole was worth it.

"No problem, Ms. Adams. That's why I come to all of my closings. Your escrow account is for your taxes and insurance. The sum of
money that you see on this line is really *your* money that's sitting in
an account with the bank *on your behalf.* When it's time to pay your
annual taxes and insurance, the bank pays it for you. Each month,
you put money into this account with your total monthly payment
to replenish the balance. You'll always be able to track this online,
and you won't have to worry about coming up with this money later."

"Oh, that's right." Ms. Adams nodded meekly.

The title agent prompted Ms. Adams to sign on the line and continued
shuffling through the mountain of papers required for a home mortgage.

Mark went into a paper trance. *It's ridiculous how much paper you have
to sign for a mortgage, no matter how big or small the loan is. There'd be no less
than a hundred papers, and that was if you didn't have a government loan! Heck,
I've received multiple offers for credit cards and lines of credit in the last month for
thirty to fifty thousand dollars, and all I had to do was give a few bits of personal
information! And what could go ever wrong with that type of lending?*

His mind continued to wander until his left jacket pocket vibrated
against his chest. An e-mail. Then another, and yet another. *Great.* Stealing
a glance, Mark saw the automatic e-mails that had just been sent from his
LOS, signaling that a file had been underwritten but that it had been suspended.

A suspended file didn't worry him too much. He prided himself on his
track record to unsuspend a file and have it close and purchased without any
issues from the investor. But the timing of this particular suspension worried
him. He'd submitted this loan a few days ago for a clear-to-close and the
underwriter was a bit bogged down. Because of that, he was beginning to
push up against his closing date, and he feared he would have another mad
scramble to get to closing. With any luck, the borrower wouldn't be any the
wiser and he could pull this off with minimal damage. He'd done it before.
But luck was a rare commodity in his life lately, and he felt his was running
thin. He tried to stay off the phone during closings, but this was a bit urgent.

Mark swiped the screen with his thumb and accessed his e-mail without looking at the phone. He put the phone beside him on the table so that he could focus on the e-mail and appear engaged in the closing. Sure enough, it was the Brown file.

This file was supposed to be a slam dunk, but it'd been plagued with annoying issues from the get-go. Mark discreetly scanned through the underwriting conditions. The underwriter reported that the DTI was too high, the borrower didn't have enough funds for closing, and there was a repair issue on the house that needed to be addressed.

A small bead of sweat formed on Mark's temple. *How could this be?* These were fairly serious issues that he hadn't seen at all when they'd submitted for the clear-to-close. Surely the underwriter had seen the bump in income? He briefly thought of his plan to call more prospects that morning and winced—yet another unmet goal. No doubt he'd be on the phone to handle this latest crisis the moment Ms. Adams finished signing her mountain of documents.

So much for making my calls. So much for ever staying on schedule.

The closing continued without many more questions. Mark gave a brief nod and a grin when Ms. Adams would look up for direction. She did seem genuinely happy, and Mark was happy for her. He tried to keep his mind on the closing at hand. When they were done signing, Ms. Adams gave him a big hug, and Mark walked her to her little red Honda Civic with a few door dings dotting the driver side. She gingerly backed out of her parking spot and rolled down her window to give him a final wave. Mark faked a smile and waved back in return as her Honda drove away. When she was out of sight, Mark scanned the lot for his car. It was all he could do to keep from sprinting.

Once in his car, he immediately called the underwriter, but she was unavailable. He rubbed his temples in anticipation of her return call, then stomped on the gas. After calling his processor on the drive back to the office, his morning at the office didn't get any better. He had two more issues to resolve on other files as well. They weren't as pressing, but they were still definitely important.

The quality issues David and he had discussed were rearing their ugly heads. He still wasn't sure what was wrong on the Brown file, but his other two files had simply been poorly originated. He knew that but his pride didn't want to take responsibility for it.

Mark glanced at the whiteboard where he tracked his fundings and at what stage his files were at in the manufacturing process. *It's still early in the month, but I can already tell it's not going to be as good as I want. May not even be as good as I need—not unless I really double down on my work. But Jennifer will blow a gasket if I do that.*

Complicating matters, he'd set a new production goal for himself following his happy hour conversation with Tyler. Mark had no idea how he was going to get there, but he wanted to hit it. *If Tyler could do it, surely he could as well, right?* That conversation was all he had thought about over the weekend. *Thirty units. Thirty units! With a team!* Mark could barely manage his own pipeline of five to seven units.

Then there was this Miracle Morning business. He'd done some initial research online about who the author was and what the method entailed. It didn't immediately grab him.

How could waking up a little earlier in the morning and spending an hour doing six different things really make that big of a difference?

The desk phone next to him lit up. Mark grabbed it like a lifeline. In his calmest voice he said, "This is Mark."

"Hey Mark, it's Teri. I listened to your voicemail, but I think we've still got a problem."

Of course we have a problem, Ms. Underwriter who takes far too long to call me back. You're too strict!

"I'm not sure what the issue could be, Teri. I triple-checked this file. I've read the guidelines, and I'm confident that all the issues, outside of the needed repairs, are resolved."

"The problem is with the mileage you tried to add back. This is an FH . . ."

"I can prove to you that we can add the mileage back into the income calculation. It's in the Fannie guides!" Mark interrupted, exasperated.

"That's the problem, Mark." Teri's voice rose as she was clearly frustrated over being interrupted. "As I was saying, this is an FHA loan. While many of the guidelines are similar, FHA does not explicitly follow the mileage deduction rules that the Fannie guides outline. None of our investors are going to allow this income."

Mark jerked the phone away from his ear and held it over his head, fighting the urge to slam the receiver back into its place. *How did I mess up a detail like that?* His mind raced, but Mortgage Mark's calm voice came through. "Wow, you're right. I completely overlooked that. What are my options?"

"Well, the good news is, you're not that far off on the income. We'll have the processor order a few supplements to see if any of the payments are actually lower than what's reported. Additionally, I saw that there were three auto loans in their name. In my experience, that typically means they assisted with the loan, but aren't making payments. If you can prove that someone else has made the payments on one of those auto loans, that'll do the trick."

Mark's breathing returned to near-normal. *Good observation, Teri, but I could have sworn I asked about this when I first sent you the application.* He clicked through the conversation notes in his LOS, but he didn't see any mention of the auto loans. "That's great. Thank you, Teri. Now, what are your concerns with the funds to close?"

"I'm pretty concerned about this one, Mark. Since these borrowers are self-employed and are using funds from their business for the down payment, I have to justify to myself, the investor, and FHA that this will not cause their business to struggle. What if the borrowers miss a mortgage payment because their business account was depleted?"

"Okay, I know, I read the guidelines here. It's allowed for sure," Mark quickly rebutted.

"Yeah, you're right, Mark, but it's ultimately the underwriter's call because I have to put my name on these findings. You didn't put any sort of support in the file as to why this would be a good underwriting decision. Please get with the borrowers and gather as much documentation as you can to support that their down payment will not put their business in a tough position."

"Teri, I don't want to sound rude, but I'm literally *days* away from closing. It's not realistic for you to be requesting this kind of information *this close* to closing. What if they can't produce exactly what you're looking for? What's good enough? It's very subjective!" Mark's frustration and panic had crept back into his voice.

"Mark, you're not making things any easier by getting upset. You're right, it is subjective, but that's why you're the loan officer putting these deals together. It's *your* responsibility to analyze the borrower's scenario and make sure that you're structuring the right deal for them. I won't waive this condition, even if that means we miss the closing date or don't close this loan at all."

"Okay, I'll shoulder *my responsibility* and get the documents from them. Thanks for your time." Mark lifted the receiver above his head again, but this time he completed the motion his body, mind, and soul yearned to commit. In quick succession, he slammed the receiver down three separate times.

Triple-check that, Teri!

Two of his colleagues turned around in their chairs and peered into his office through the glass wall. He knew it was stupid to get upset with Teri. She was only doing her job, and he had made some missteps on this file that he shouldn't have. Plus, she was the gatekeeper and he'd just pissed her off by acting immaturely. Mark took a few breaths to calm himself and called his processor.

"Linda, it's Mark. We need to scramble on this Brown file."

"Hey, Mark. I'm a bit slammed with a few files. I'm not sure I can push them aside for your file right now."

"We can take care of these conditions, but we have to act right now. Will you please help me? We'll miss the closing date otherwise." *The opening magic words of a loan officer in need.*

Mark heard Linda sigh. There was a long pause on the other end. Finally, Linda replied, "Fine Mark, I'll make this a priority, but it puts me in a tough spot. I'm probably going to have to work late to catch up on the other files so that we keep moving along."

"I know, Linda, and I'm sorry. I'll make it up to you." *The closing magic words of a loan officer in need.*

Mark spent the next fifteen minutes filling Linda in on his conversation with Teri and creating a plan to clear the conditions that were hindering the Brown file from closing. By the time he hung up the phone, he could tell that his entire day was going to be spent trying to get this loan closed. Hours meant everything at this point. Even if he had to go to his borrower's business and hand-deliver what needed to be taken care of, he would. He was well known for this personal touch to get files closed, but it often meant he was less productive that month.

The rest of the day went exactly as Mark had predicted: poorly. By 6:00 that evening, he'd managed to get everything resolved on the Brown file, but it had taken him the entire day to do so and he had created additional stress for his entire production team. He would have to call Teri tomorrow and apologize and bring Linda her favorite Starbucks. This is getting so old.

CHAPTER 6
BROODING IN THE BATCAVE

As he sat in his car outside of his home, he felt completely spent. This wasn't fun. This wasn't what he enjoyed doing. He had more days like this one than he cared to remember. Not only was it draining him, but it often crept into his home life. He would brood during dinner or wouldn't have the energy to give Jason the attention he deserved. On top of that, Jennifer deserved better. Despite the distance he knew was growing between them, she would still put on a smile and happily meet him at the door when he walked in, grateful that he was home so that they could spend at least time together.

What in the world had he done to marry such a catch? She was out of his league, not only physically, but mentally too. Mark shook his head to clear his thoughts. He didn't know much about self-improvement, but he knew enough to keep himself from dwelling in negativity. Mark gathered his things and made his way to the front door. Jingling the house keys and fumbling for the keyhole, Boomer went ballistic on the other side of the door. Surely their English bulldog knew it was him by now. They'd had him since he was a puppy, and for the last two years, Mark had come home about the same time every day. Almost no one but Mark ever used the front door.

Are you impaired, Boomer?

The dog often stared at walls for minutes at a time, inches away from the drywall. Mark finally got the keys in the door and instinctively kicked at the opening to keep Boomer from streaking out. That's the last thing he needed after today. After a second or two, Boomer realized the boogie man wasn't breaking in and stopped barking. The dog's stubby tail wiggled furiously as he waited for Mark to set his things down and give him his daily rubdown. Mark hated and loved this ritual. Boomer's grunting noises always made him smile, but the dog always stunk. Even after weekly baths and numerous medications, the dog's coat was perpetually rancid. Through the snorting, Mark heard Jennifer shuffling down the hallway on cue. She smiled when she saw him. He felt his mood lighten even more.

"Hey baby, how was your day?" Jennifer nudged Boomer out of the way and embraced Mark. Mark wiped the dog hair off his hands and wrapped his arms around his wife, pulling her head into the crook of his neck. He took a deep breath and asked, "How did you know?"

Jennifer looked up at him with a slight smile. "It's in your eyes. They look tired and worried." She only hugged him like that when she knew he needed it. Mark embraced her again and rested his head on hers.

What a blessing to have this kind of support.

He knew plenty of other men who didn't have this kind of love waiting for them when they got home. Jennifer never let him forget how much she appreciated him fighting for the well-being of their family.

She traced the bag beneath his left eye. "Was it as tough a day as you look?"

"Yes, unfortunately. I'll fill you in later. How's dinner coming along? I'm starving!"

"It'll be done in just a few minutes. Bacon-wrapped shrimp and angel hair pasta."

"Hmm, that sounds great, hon. Just what I need. Where's Jason?"

"He's building a space agency out of Legos upstairs. Watch your feet. I took an alien right to the arch of my foot this morning. Our son almost learned a new four-letter word."

Or one he's probably already learned from me.

Mark chuckled and started toward the stairs, sweeping the ground with his eyes. He was all too familiar with the indescribable pain of hard plastic Legos crunched beneath bare feet. Near the top of the stairs he heard his son scraping through plastic bins.

He must have close to a million pieces.

For a kid his age, Jason was surprisingly fascinated with space. Mark didn't care much for it, but Jason had latched on to space exploration after watching a movie about a kid who partners with an alien to save Earth from an asteroid.

Mark paused in the doorway and silently watched his little architect at work. Jason moved nimbly from one bin to the next. Mark hadn't noticed before, but it looked like Jason had actually taken the time to sort the pieces by color and type. *Who was this kid?* At his son's age, Mark was pretty sure he was eating his own boogers and mindlessly watching TV. After a minute, Mark could tell Jason was struggling to find a particular piece. Mark didn't have the mind to construct ships and buildings, but he was happy to be Jason's assistant as he hunted for what he was looking for.

"Hey buddy, can I help you find a piece?"

"Hi, Dad! Yeah, I need help. I can't find what I'm looking for. I know it's here, but there's just so many pieces."

"No problem." Mark crouched down next to Jason and looked at what he was building—some sort of ship likely designed by Picasso, judging by its various levels and awkward angles. From what he could tell, Jason was just about done with the cockpit. "What do you need next?"

"I need a piece to put the window on. You know, like a door arm. So it can open and close."

The grammar was a little off, but Mark got the picture. He rummaged through the nearest bin filled with all sorts of white pieces. Jason noticed where he was looking and scrunched up his nose, clearly displeased. "What's up, bud?"

"It needs to be red. See, the ship is blue and red. If it's white, it'll look funny." Jason moved over to the red bin and hoisted it into his little arms, nearly dropping the entire bin. Mark started to lunge forward to help, but caught himself. He didn't want to jump in too quickly. Failing wasn't a bad thing, and the image of thousands of pieces piling onto his little engineer would have been a cherished memory and story. Jason managed to shift the weight of the bin so he wasn't off balance and proudly marched over to his dad. Mark smiled and pinched his son's biceps as he laid the bin back down. "Man, you're going to be stronger than me soon!" Jason beamed and tried to flex his arms.

"Hey boys, time for dinner!" Jennifer called from the base of the stairs.

"Ugh, do we have to?" Jason whined.

"Yep, the chef is calling us. We mustn't keep her. Go wash up and wait for me to go downstairs. We'll keep working after dinner for a little while before you go to bed."

"Oh, okay." Jason shuffled reluctantly toward the bathroom with a little sigh, not happy with the delay to his project. Mark followed him out and moved on to the master bedroom. After changing into shorts and a T-shirt, he met Jason at the stairs. Walking side by side, they made their way into the kitchen. Jennifer was just laying the shrimp and pasta on to the kitchen table.

"Oh my God," Mark called out. "You've created a masterpiece!"

"Yeah, yeah, sweet talker. Sit down and bless the food."

As Mark cleared the plates after dinner, he realized he'd been so entranced by his wife's eyes and engaged by his son's plans to complete his ship that he hadn't thought about work for at least thirty minutes.

Well, at least I hadn't thought about work until I thought about the fact that I hadn't thought about it.

Mark walked Jason back to his room, where they spent some more time working on the rocket ship. Mark read the latest *Magic School Bus* book to Jason until he fell asleep. Of course, the book was a constant favorite because it was about space. Mark lifted himself off Jason's bed and kissed his son's head softly before tucking him in and walking out of the room.

Before Mark made his way to the master, he made his nightly sweep of the house. He set the alarm and checked the front and back doors, Boomer in tow. God help him if an intruder came in with Boomer nearby. That dog was worthless when it came to defense. He'd probably break his neck tripping over the darn dog. Satisfied that the house was locked down, he made his way back up to the master bedroom.

The weight of the day creeped back into his mind. He did his best to force the negative thoughts and frustrations away during dinner and his time with Jason, but it was tough. He really felt that he was struggling with a fundamental core of his job. If he was making mistakes and getting sloppy, he had no one to blame but himself. *How hard is it to fill out a 1003? It's not rocket science! It's only three to four pages and literally takes fifteen to twenty minutes to fill out.* Maybe he was getting too confident. Maybe his years in the business were actually beginning to work against him because he wasn't thinking everything through.

As he walked into their room, Jennifer glanced up from her book and asked, "Okay, what's wrong. Is everything okay at work?"

Wow, I've completely lost my poker face. Or maybe I've just never had one with Jennifer.

"Yeah, everything's okay. Nothing life-threatening."

"That's comforting." Jennifer smirked. "Seriously, what's up? You're brooding more than usual. You're reminding me of Bruce

Wayne in his Batcave, all dark and serious." She frowned and tilted her head down, squinting at Mark. He couldn't help but smirk back.

"I'm worried I'm losing my touch. I'm struggling to keep up with everything that I've got going on and I'm making mistakes that I shouldn't. Mistakes that could keep my clients from getting into homes on time. Mistakes that could cost me referral relationships. You know I'm only as good as my last closed loan."

Jennifer furrowed her brow. "That sounds a little more serious than I thought."

"It is and it isn't. I think all LOs struggle with this, but I didn't think it would happen to me. I almost had the Brown loan die on me today and it's supposed to close in a few days. I had to scramble and save face with them, but I lost some respect and trust from my team. I forced them to clean up my mess at the expense of others. That doesn't fly for very long."

"Is everything going to be okay income wise?"

"Yeah, really, everything is fine. I know we've had some ups and downs recently, but I've got a handle on this." *What a lie. I'm flying by the seat of my pants. But why should Jennifer fret about things she can't control? This is on me. I need to fix it.* "I just need to get back to the basics and clean up my processes."

Looking more distressed than before, Jennifer responded with a simple, "Okay." She patted the bed next to her, indicating her desire that Mark fulfill his cuddle duties. Mark obliged and laid down. She rolled over where she was partially laying on his chest and stomach. He lightly stroked her hair, working to clear his thoughts so he could sleep. If he wasn't careful, he'd have another ESPN night.

She broke their sleepy silence. "I meant to ask you the other night, how's Tyler doing?"

Yes, Tyler. I'm sure he's doing fine, closing his thirty loans a month and making half a mil!

Mark had briefly mentioned that he saw Tyler at the networking event, but he and Jennifer had never talked about it. Mark gave her the play-by-play on their conversation. Her eyes widened when he mentioned how many loans Tyler and his team were doing.

Guess I'll get to find out what's on ESPN tonight after all.

Jennifer's reaction showed that she was clearly impressed with Tyler's success in the last few years. When he mentioned the Miracle Morning Tyler had started, her eyes widened again. "He wakes up *before* five a.m. every morning? How?"

"I don't know, but I don't plan on starting," Mark quickly replied. He couldn't tell if she was fishing for this or not, but anything that would take more time away from her and Jason probably wasn't going to happen. Her next question surprised him though.

"Does he really think it's helping him hit those numbers?"

Where is she going with this?

"Yeah, he said it was a game-changer for him. I don't really know what that means. I looked into the book a little bit, but I wasn't impressed. More of the same visualizations, affirmations, meditation kind of stuff. You know, the stuff that makes those authors a boatload of money but doesn't really help the reader."

"Hmm, maybe. Karen told me that her vision board is what helped her lose all that weight."

"Karen lost that weight because the divorce forced her back on to the market." The words were out of his mouth before he could filter them.

Jennifer looked up at him with disapproval. "That was really rude, Mark Stiles. You know she took the divorce hard." She shook her head and rolled over, taking half the covers with her. She topped off the move with a heavy sigh.

It was out of line, but he didn't feel like saying sorry. After the split, Karen had ended up staying at their house for two of the longest nights in recent memory. She did nothing but wail endlessly in the guest bedroom next door. After the day he'd had, he just wanted to go to sleep and start over. His heart raced and sleep was nowhere to be found. His mind frantically relived every mistake he'd ever made. He then found himself doing a quick mental review of their finances (which made his heart race even faster.) He then thought about this so-called Miracle Morning. At that point, he knew sleep was out of the question so he quietly got up and trudged back downstairs.

The instant his bare foot came down on the first stair, Mark experienced a sudden flashback of terror while envisioning all the covert Legos strewn all over the house, each lurking in hidden minefields just waiting for its next inevitable victim. His autopilot body moved faster than his sleepy mind and all of his weight came down on a half-inch block. Oh, my God, the pain was excruciating! *Dear God, I can't scream and have Boomer go ballistic and wake up Jennifer.* In his head, Mark screamed every obscenity at the top of his lungs but at the top of the stairs, he managed to stifle his agony and reduce his imaginary screams to deep, guttural groans.

Holding his throbbing foot in his palm as though in a yoga pose, he picked up the Lego and threw it across the hallway toward Jason's room. He felt a little better taking his anger out on the wall, but his foot was on fire. He limped into the living room and flipped on the TV. After a few minutes of watching talking heads, he got bored and grabbed his iPad off the living room table. Facebook and YouTube didn't hold their usual interest, either. Mark couldn't contain it any longer. He had to reach out to Tyler.

Tyler had clearly figured out something Mark hadn't. Whether it was a Miracle Morning, a new sales technique, his new company or something completely out of the box, Mark had to figure it out. He couldn't handle this roller coaster anymore—the months of meager, lonely frustration had to stop. He hated never being sure about his production. He hated constantly putting out fires. It was time for a change.

Mark typed in Tyler's e-mail address and paused at the subject line. He attempted a few eloquent lines, but eventually settled on "Help!" Mark typed feverishly, even cathartically. In a few paragraphs, he poured out his frustrations, what was happening in his business, and ended with a simple cry for help:

"I don't know exactly how you've managed your success, but I know it's different than what I'm doing. If you're willing to help, I'd be eternally grateful."

Mark rubbed his foot as he read over the message a few times, then he hit "Send."

Mark set the tablet next to him, feeling a little better. A minute or two passed and Mark heard the familiar ding of a return message. He tapped the power button on the iPad.

11:30 p.m. Surely I don't have a response already. Doesn't he have to get up before five tomorrow?

Sure enough, Tyler had responded with a few short sentences.

I'd be happy to help. Call you in the morning. Get some sleep!

Mark smirked at the irony of getting sleep when Tyler was supposed to be waking up in a few short hours, but he heeded Tyler's advice and headed up to bed.

But as soon as Mark laid his head on his pillow, the thought struck him: *Is he going to call when his morning starts, or mine?*

CHAPTER 7
THE TIPPING POINT

Tyler's late night message had done little for Mark's peace of mind. Those short sentences were like a shot of espresso. He had lain in bed for hours thinking about what advice he'd be given and what his life might look like if he wasn't facing one problem after another all the time. Mark's alarm blared at 6:30 a.m. and had promptly been snoozed. Five snoozes later, Jennifer was shoving him out of bed at 7:15 a.m. He was in an absolute fog, and when he felt like this it always took twice as long to get moving and out the door. Mark got to the office just fifteen minutes later than usual, a large coffee in hand.

He wasn't sure when Tyler would call, but the combination of being tired and the excuse of keeping the lines free left him one clear option: web surfing. He knew he should be productive regardless of how much time he had, but his willpower was nowhere to be found. Finally, an hour later, the phone rang.

Give it three rings. If it's Tyler, let's not appear too desperate.

"This is Mortgage Mark."

"Hey Mortgage Mark, it's Tyler. Nice title. How's that been working for you?"

"Better than you might think. It helps me to stay top of mind with acquaintances and networkers," Mark replied, hoping it didn't sound lame.

"Whatever works! There was an LO at the Todd Duncan conference a few years ago who was known as "The Mortgage Geek". She said it helped her get more business, and she created a library of videos online with that persona. With that and a few other strategies, she increased her fundings by about fifteen million dollars."

A low "wow" escaped Mark's lips. *I can't imagine increasing my business by that much.* "For these LOs at the Todd Duncan conference, what does their production look like?"

"It tends to be the best of the best. Usually LOs that have a finely tuned business plan and a consistent execution strategy. The top originator and his team completed three hundred and thirty-four units for sixty-seven million dollars last year." Tyler never missed a beat, but Mark's mind was swimming, trying to wrap his mind around that level of production.

" . . . and then this originator in Alabama . . ." Tyler continued, oblivious to Mark's lack of attention.

"Sorry, Tyler, let me interrupt you for just a second. Do you really think that this person did that kind of production or do you think that it was a tactic on Duncan's part to get people to believe in his methods. Maybe someone just planted in the audience?"

"Man, you're still as skeptical as you used to be. It's the real deal. You seem to be getting hung up on what other people are producing. How do you feel about your production?"

Mark sat in silence a few moments before answering. "If I'm being completely honest, I'm not sure how I feel exactly. Part of me is content with where I've been and how I'm doing. I have the money I need to pay my bills with a little extra left over. But when I hear about how you're doing and these other originators, I realize how much potential there is in this business. I want a bigger slice of the pie."

"Yeah, it can be tough digging deep into your thoughts and figuring out priorities. I sometimes still struggle with it myself. It's all about priorities and strategies, Mark. Do you have a strategy? I've met some originators that are happy as clams producing five or six loans a month. But it doesn't sound like you're very happy with how things are going. In fact, it doesn't sound like you're very happy with much of ANYTHING this morning."

Is it that obvious?

Mark rubbed his eyes and took a breath. "I guess you're right. I'm not happy with how things are going. When I can produce eight to ten loans a month—which is a massive month for me—it's an absolute scramble. I feel like I'm holding the pieces together with a shoestring and everything's ready to unravel at the slightest tug. Then the next month or two are pretty meager as I have to ramp up my pipeline again. Plus, the week after a big month I just don't have any motivation because I think, 'Is it worth it to go through that again?' Then the bills start coming in and I get my butt into gear. It's an endless cycle."

The last sentence came out pretty weakly.

Mark, why are you being so honest with someone you've grown apart from over the years? You haven't even been that real with yourself lately!

"Whoa, are you sure you're okay? Do you still enjoy doing this?" Tyler asked.

"Yeah, I'm doing okay. Just some days I ask whether or not it's worth it. The constant struggle to get business and then to turn around and get those loans closed without ruining relationships just wears on me. The irony is, I couldn't imagine doing anything different though. The money is too good and I don't know where else I'd get this kind of flexibility."

That's sadly true, every word of it.

"What does Jennifer think?"

The question caught Mark off guard.

What does *Jennifer think? She's always so supportive of me, but based on the ways she's looked at me the last few days . . .*

"I really don't know, Tyler. I haven't asked her in years. She's supportive of me. I think she likes the flexibility. But . . ."

"But what?" Tyler pressed.

"I suppose I abuse the flexibility every once in a while. I'm physically present with her and Jason, but my mind wanders toward my work or I'm on my phone." He grimaced at the memory of missing Jason's game a few days ago. Jennifer's look had almost killed him. And their arguments were becoming far too similar and all too frequent. He'd always tell her that he was working on it, but he didn't have anything to show—and she knew it. *Yet she stays.*

"Hmm. I suppose we can pick that up later. Oh, geez, I've only got fifteen minutes."

Fifteen minutes?! I stayed up half the night wondering what the conversation would bring and all I get is an e-therapy session. I don't even feel any better!

Tyler didn't let the silence linger. "Mark, you mentioned something a while ago that I think is pretty key. Why do you feel you struggle with your closings?"

"I'm not sure you have enough time for that, Tyler." It was a defeated response, but he was being honest.

"Hit me. Let's see what you've got."

Mark's verbal floodgates opened again. "Geez, where do I start? Maybe my borrowers. I tell them everything that I need up front and they drag their feet for days or weeks before I get everything. When I do get documents things are missing or illegible. Then when I tell them something isn't quite right they get upset that I've made their lives more difficult. Then I dump everything into the file and send it off to my processor. But she's usually backed up with all of her other files so it takes a few days for my loan to go into the underwriter. I have to stay on her to keep things moving along because by the time it goes into the underwriter I usually only have two weeks left on the contract. The underwriter is pretty fast but between other rush files that sometimes get pushed ahead of mine or last-minute revisions for loans trying to close, I often experience delays which I then have to explain to everybody. It just takes too long in my opinion. I get the conditions back and run to my borrowers again, praying they listen to me and get everything back in a timely manner. Then, it's back on the merry-go-round again, sending the next slew of documents and explanations back to my processor and begging her to get the file resubmitted ASAP. At this point, the fervent prayers begin that the underwriter doesn't ask for anything else. While all of this is going on, I'm still trying to make my prospecting calls, meeting with pro-spective borrowers, and attending networking events."

"And finding time for your family."

"Of course. That's a given."

"Is it?"

Silence.

Tyler was the first to speak. "I'm sorry. I shouldn't have said that."

"Can we just focus on the work right now?"

"Sure. I apologize. Not my place. But I do know loans. Do you have a dedicated processor?" Tyler started launching a salvo of questions.

"No, but probably eighty percent of her files are mine."

Tyler paused. "And do the other LOs have problems getting loans closed on time?"

"Uh, I don't know. I don't think they have the same problems. At least I don't hear about them." Mark knew where this question was going. He shot a question back, a little irritated.

"You're saying the problem is with me?"

"No, I'm just asking questions. What does your communication look like with the realtor?"

"I keep them updated on big milestones and let them know when we have a clear-to-close. I make sure to keep my borrower's information private."

"I agree that you shouldn't overshare, but you may not be communicating with the realtor enough. Does the realtor know when you have issues getting things from the borrower?"

"No, I don't want them to think I can't do my job!" Mark tried to blink away his weariness and mounting anger. *Get a grip. He's just trying to help.*

"Mark, I'm not trying to make you look bad. I'm just trying to get to the bottom of what you're struggling with. Would you rather we not do this exercise?"

"No, of course not. I'm clearly struggling. I'm sorry, I didn't sleep well last night and I'm flustered with the files that I've got going on right now."

"Okay, well, I've only got five minutes left and we're certainly not going to solve problems in this conversation. I honestly wasn't sure what to expect and thought you just had questions about my routines and the Miracle Morning."

"Tyler, I didn't know what to expect either. I certainly didn't intend to lie on a leather couch."

"Let me leave you with two things and then let's plan on talking this weekend. First, Todd Duncan's conference is at the end of the month. I highly recommend that you attend and hear the success stories of other originators. He also brings in phenomenal guest speakers."

"But, Tyler, that's at the end of the month. I can't leave my loans."

"I know it's at the end of the month, but you want to change the way things are going for you, right? Or, do you really want to keep doing your business this way?"

"Okay, I'll look into it." Mark wasn't sure if he would actually look into it or not, but he wanted to hear what the second thing was before Tyler had to go.

"No, you'll go or I'm not going to help you."

Who does this guy think he is? And why do I keep listening to him? He's never talked to me this way before. I haven't been talked to like this by anyone before. But how can I argue? Tyler's successful. I'm not.

"Okay, I'll commit to going this month."

"Good. Now, here's the second thing and then I *have* to go. Today, on your way home from work, stop in at the bookstore and pick up a copy of *The Miracle Morning*. I want us to talk about it this weekend. If you haven't read the book, there's no point in us talking."

Mark was at his limit with the commands. "Tyler, I've had enough of you dictating to me what I'm going to do and when I'm going to do it. I reached out to you because you're a friend. I was hoping that you'd have some techniques to share that helped you get where you're at. I can't possibly understand how this book is going to help me."

"Mark, I AM your friend, but my time is too precious to waste on someone that's not going to do what it takes to succeed. You're the one that called me for help, remember? I know we go a ways back and we've drifted apart, but I truly want you to be successful. Reach out to me if you pick up the book. If you don't read it before this weekend, there's no reason for us to meet again. I have to go now."

With that, the line went dead. Stunned, Mark sat in silence with the receiver still in his hand. He snapped out of his funk when the line started beeping indicating that the receiver was still off the base.

"What the hell just happened?" Mark wondered aloud.

He couldn't believe the direction the conversation had taken. Tyler had essentially accused him of causing his own problems and then called him a waste of time. For the next thirty minutes, Mark stared out his frosted office window. The conversation played over and over in his mind.

If he was being perfectly honest, he didn't have a good handle on what it took to get a loan done the right way anymore. He was so set in his ways that after he requested the standard income, credit, and asset documents, he was on autopilot and he expected someone else down the chain to take over. If he didn't get something right, someone else down the line would fix it.

Geez, that just sounds wrong and even somewhat lazy. But is it, really?

If he was busy chasing down documents and analyzing every piece of documentation that came through, he and the company would starve. He was a rainmaker. The hunter. If he didn't kill, the tribe didn't eat. But he didn't used to have these problems.

When he had less production and was still learning the ropes of the business, he had been terrified to make a mistake and ruin a relationship. He would work on a file for hours trying to consider all the angles and make sure that he had everything up front. It was exhausting, both for him and his borrowers, but there wasn't this last-minute madness that seemed to be his new standard. Mark pondered this for a few minutes before his office phone rang. "Mark, it's Linda. Do you have a second?"

Linda the loan processor. What fresh hell is coming my way now?

CHAPTER 8
QUALITY CONTROL

M ark's heart beat a little faster. "Uh, sure Linda. Is there something on one of our files?"

"Yeah, but it should be pretty minor. Nothing that would cause us not to be approved, but conditions all the same. I called the Smiths just a few minutes ago to request some of the conditions we needed. I was promptly informed by the borrowers that they didn't know who I was and didn't feel comfortable sending me information without speaking with you first. When I told them what I needed, they got a little more upset because they said they'd already provided this to you a few weeks ago. Sorry to bother you with this, but I need help."

Mark took a deep breath and held it for a few seconds. *A little brain damage, but not a crisis.* He went through the list of conditions with Linda. Sure enough, the Smiths had sent those files and Mark had thrown them into a folder in Outlook. At the time he wasn't sure if they were necessary, so he just put them aside.

"Well, the good news is I have that documentation, Linda. Do you want me to send those to you by e-mail or upload them?"

"Go ahead and e-mail them to me. I prefer for them to be up-loaded so I don't have to do extra work, but I'm working on this one right now anyway." Linda paused for a few minutes. Silence lingered until Mark broke it.

"Is there something else, Linda?"

"Well, I hate to bring this up, but we talked about this very issue last month. Remember our agreement for you to upload everything you get from the borrowers and let me sort through it? Or did you just forget?"

Mark sensed her frustration but didn't appreciate her condescension. She didn't work directly for him, but he was a source of her income. In a sense, she did rely on him.

She must be pretty upset to be so forward.

"Honestly Linda, I forgot that you wanted to see all the documentation from the borrowers. I wasn't sure what was and wasn't important, so I just threw in the normal stuff. Pay stubs, tax returns, bank statements—"

"I understand Mark, but that was the whole purpose of our last thirty-minute discussion. After those files blew up at the last minute, we talked about ways to prevent that from happening again in the future. Well, now we're in the future and it's still happening with little change. From now on—"

"Linda, I really don't appreciate you going off on me like this. If you're not happy with how this is working, I can find another processor."

Mark's ego swelled at that last comment. He hoped it had sounded threatening enough that the conversation would change directions.

"Mark, you changing processors would be an absolute blessing for me!"

Did she seriously just say what I think she said?

"I don't want to be rude but the last six months of working on your files has been nothing but a nightmare. Half the time, I don't even want to go to work because you're my highest producing loan officer. Do you know why I'm your processor?"

She didn't hesitate to answer her own question. "It wasn't because Sara wanted to move to a different team. She was on the verge of quitting. Well, now I'm in the same spot, so good luck trying to get another processor. As far as I can tell, I'm it!"

Mark's cheeks flushed. He was too ashamed to fire back. The implications of what Linda said were pretty big. If processors were being reassigned so that the company didn't lose valued employees, it meant his name was a mockery throughout the company.

The processors talked among themselves about the files they worked on and how things were going. These processors talked to the underwriters about their frustrations. Mark was convinced his work was public knowledge.

I must have been kidding myself these past months. What I thought wasn't too bad must be a good deal more severe. Is this why my branch manager has been on my case so much?

Sensing his discomfort, Linda tried to lessen the blow. "Look Mark, I didn't mean to go off like that. It wasn't professional, and I should have left it up to David to talk to you. I like you as a person, but you're killing me with the subpar work you've been turning in. Let's just end this conversation now and we'll figure out where to go from here. Okay?"

Mark's response was quiet and humbled, "Okay. I just sent the files."

Mark hung up and stared out the window. A hollow and vacant feeling washed over him as he digested where things stood. Some time later, Mark spotted David walking through the office, drinking coffee and stopping to chat with the operations staff in their cubes.

I need to talk to David immediately. I can get the lowdown and see if things are really that bad. God, the last thing I need is to get canned.

Firing an LO for anything but an egregious offense was rare, but his company had done it before. Taking a deep breath to steady his voice, Mark stuck his head out of his office.

"Hey David, do you have a few minutes to talk?"

David looked up and waved. He talked for a few minutes to Jessica, the internal funder, then walked toward Mark. It wasn't a far walk, but it felt like ages.

"Hey Mark, what's up? Your face is flushed. Everything okay?"

"Yeah, I'm fine, but I'd like to talk for a few minutes in your office. Is now a good time?"

"Uh." David glanced down at his smart phone and clicked to his calendar. "I've got fifteen minutes before a corporate call. Is that enough time?"

"Should be. I just need to get some feedback from you."

"Okay, let's head that way."

Walking side by side, they chatted on the short walk to David's office at the corner of the suite, a typical manager's office in Dallas, the kind with an open floor plan and a ridiculous amount of unused space. Rich, dark wood bordered the floor boards and ceiling. An equally rich floor-to-ceiling bookcase was filled with all sorts of books from *The Art of War* to *The Goal*. Mark wondered if David had actually read these books or if they were simply for show.

Mark respected David for the most part, but David had very little experience in mortgage originations. Mark found it hard to take direction from someone whom he outranked in the trenches. According to everyone in the office, David had been asked to move in to a management role because of his tactics and ability to lead, but Mark just didn't see it. He felt like David could come off as a blowhard more often than being a relatable human being. Still, most people in the office respected David and genuinely seemed to like him.

Maybe I can add that to my growing list of problems to discuss with Tyler: how to look like you actually like your boss.

Two plush black leather chairs sat opposite of David's oversized desk. After taking a seat, David began.

"Mark, it seems like something's bothering you. I'm not sure if we can completely resolve it right now, but let's give it a shot."

That sounded eerily like Tyler.

Mark let out a barely audible laugh. "Yeah, I had a very concerning call with Linda just now. We started out talking about a particular file and then the conversation turned into a bit of a trial regarding our work relationship."

"Oh?" David seemed genuinely surprised.

"She said that she'd been really frustrated by quality issues on my files and that Sara was reassigned to another pool of LOs so that the company wouldn't lose her. Linda indicated that she'd had about enough of me as well."

David leaned back in his chair and lightly stroked the hair on his chin. Wanting to break the awkward silence, Mark continued.

"I know I've been facing some issues and we've talked about this over the last few months, but I didn't know my work was having this sort of impact on the team. Is what Linda said true?"

David sat up and looked at his ridiculously large and ornate wall clock. "We don't have enough time to give this conversation justice, but yes, there have been some discussions between upper-level management and the operations team regarding the problems that your loans are causing in the system. It is true that we had to reassign Sara because she walked into my office with a resignation letter and said she was quitting. We managed to keep her on by shuffling some people around. Linda needed some more production and thought that she could right the ship."

David paused, searching for the right words.

"Mark, your production does meaningfully contribute to the bottom line, but it's not absolutely necessary. While it would be a setback to lose you, we've been studying the impact that your loan files have on the manufacturing process. Did you know that your files take an extra hour and a half on average to underwrite?"

Crap.

"Uh, no I wasn't aware of that."

"Did you also know that your average resubmissions into underwriting are about one more on average than everyone else?"

Double crap.

"No, I didn't know that either." Mark's cheeks were flushing again as his anger welled, not just at himself, but at David and the company.

"I'm not going to lie to you Mark. There have been some discussions about whether or not you're the right fit for our company. The costs are beginning to exceed the benefits of your production."

Mark held his tongue for as long as he could.

"Well, why the *hell* didn't anyone tell me it had gotten this serious? Sugarcoating it and sweeping it under the rug clearly didn't help either!"

Ever the steely manager, David didn't flinch or raise his voice. "Nobody has the time to babysit you and your files Mark. It was our belief that by speaking with you directly about the need to improve, and the apparent train wreck of your closings, this would be enough to nudge you in the right direction to avoid this conversation. Clearly we were wrong. Now if you'll excuse me, I need to get on this call. We'll talk more about this later."

Mark got up without a second's hesitation. In his mind's eye, he saw himself storming out of David's office, using a few choice hand gestures, slamming the door as hard as he could, and causing that ridiculous clock to fall and shatter. Employees from all over the office would stand in their cubicles wondering what had happened. Some would even cheer, right?

Instead, Mark walked out and softly shut the door behind him without looking back.

I'm not going to get myself fired by acting like an idiot.

No one noticed as Mark strode to his office.

I need to get out of here. I need to clear my head and try to salvage the rest of this day—before I go ballistic and do something really stupid.

CHAPTER 9
TWO MIRACLES

Mark's walk did exactly what he had hoped it would. He still felt groggy from lack of sleep, but the walk had allowed him to cool down and face facts. Things were bad and they needed to change immediately. That was obvious. Tyler was willing to help, but he wasn't going to take any of the crap that Mark had gotten used to shoveling. Mark decided to take off early, grab the book Tyler wanted him to read, spend some quality time with Jennifer and Jason, and then get to sleep early. Tomorrow would be better.

Tomorrow had to be better.

Back at his desk, he googled the nearest bookstore. A Barnes and Noble, a Half Price Books, and a local shop he didn't recognize were all within a ten-mile radius. He called Barnes and Noble only to hear an automated message that they'd closed a month ago. Half Price didn't have the book, which made him think it might actually be a book people didn't want to part with. As a last resort, he called the local book shop.

"Thanks for calling Corner Shelf. My name is Steve. How may I help you?"

"Hey Steve, I'm looking for a book called *The Miracle Morning*."

"Okay, do you know who the author is? I haven't heard of that one."

"Uh, it starts with an H. It's a bit different. Heath or Herb?"

"Hmm, okay. Is it in the religious section? It sounds like it would be a devotional."

"No, I don't think so. I think it'll be under self-help."

"Give me a moment to see if it's on our shelves."

Mark waited for a few minutes, a small amount of frustration growing within.

Why am I doing all of this for Tyler? Oh, right, I'm about to lose my job, which may even make me lose my family, which would make me lose my mind. I need some kind of—

"*Miracle Morning* by Hal Elrod! Found it! I've got our only copy in my hand, but the book is a bit beat up and there's an inscription on the jacket cover. Are you okay with that?"

"Sure. Can you reserve it for me? I'm on my way. Name's Mark Stiles."

"No problem, Mr. Stiles. We'll have it ready for you at the front desk."

Mark looked at his computer clock: 2:30 was a little early to be heading home, but with getting the book and fighting early rush-hour, he'd probably be home about 4:00 p.m. That'd be late enough not to cause a panic with Jennifer as to why he was home early.

The universe must have gotten word of the day Mark had suffered and had pity on him. Traffic was miraculous, and he got to the store easily and arrived home in record time. Pulling in next to his wife's car, Mark wasted no time getting his things together and out of his own car. He wanted to take advantage of every minute with his wife and son. Mark walked up to the front door. On cue, Boomer went berserk.

Sliding in, Mark noticed that the house was dim, quiet, and remarkably odor-free. Mark checked his watch: 4:03. It was still a little early, but he was surprised that dinner hadn't been started. Jason typically went to bed around 8:00 so dinner needed to be ready early enough to keep their schedule. Mark walked to the end of the hall and surveyed the kitchen and living room. Not only was it empty, but the lights were off.

This is weird. Something's . . . off.

Mark picked up a butcher knife from the kitchen. It was overkill to be marching around the house armed, but he didn't want to take any chances. Listening carefully, he couldn't hear a single thing from Jennifer or Jason.

Turning toward the garage, Mark stealthily walked to the laundry room. He kept the knife down and turned inward in order to avoid a horrific family stabbing like he'd heard about on the news a few weeks back. He imagined the dark headline: "Estranged loan officer stabs family after bad day at office."

The hall was dark and windowless. Briskly, Mark stepped forward and flipped the switch on. He took a step back. The florescent lights kicked on, flashing a few times, then holding steady. Everything was in place. Mark glanced at the garage door and saw that the lock was in place.

They're not out there. It's locked from the inside. What in the world is going on?

Moving back toward the kitchen, Mark heard Jason's faint voice upstairs. Listening carefully, he could tell Jason was in fantasy world, talking to himself about aliens and the moon.

At least he better be talking to himself.

Mark hid the knife inside the entry table and jogged up the stairs, taking two steps at a time. He peered into Jason's room and Jason was indeed playing alone, killer Legos scattered all around him. He then turned the opposite direction and crept towards their bedroom.

Through the crack, Mark saw that the bedroom lights were off.

Mark's brow furrowed, and for a moment he thought the unthinkable.

She wouldn't, would she? At 4 in the afternoon? With Jason home? C'mon, Mark. Get a grip. That's crazy talk. Stop being ridiculous. Although stranger things have happened.

Mark inched the door open.

The blinds were closed and the drapes were drawn. Jennifer was sitting on the edge of the bed, facing away from the door, her head low. She was looking at something in her hands. Mark heard a faint sniffle. He flipped the lights on just as Jennifer stood and faced him. She'd definitely been crying, but she was smiling too.

Mark looked at Jennifer, utterly confused.

Jennifer beamed. "Honey, we're going to have another baby."

Mark's jaw fell to the floor.

Thirty minutes ago he'd been thinking what life would be like searching for another mortgage company after being fired. Five minutes ago he'd been Black Ops Mark, searching for his family and ready to shed blood. One minute ago he'd been ready to be the next prime suspect on *Dateline*. Now, he and Jennifer were going to have another baby.

Grinning from ear to ear, he grabbed Jennifer and half-laughed, half-sobbed, "We are?"

"Uh, huh."

They embraced. He wrapped Jennifer in his arms, their tears commingling as waves of relief washed over him. She sobbed and wrapped her arms more tightly around him. That was all it took for Mark to weep without shame—an ugly, guttural cry that had been dammed for years.

They stood there for Mark didn't know how long. He didn't care. They were going to add another Stiles to the family. Nothing else mattered.

"What's wrong?" Jason stood here, holding his Lego spaceship, his little brow furrowed in confusion.

They wiped their faces and knelt down on either side of him. Mark spoke first. "These are happy tears, son. We're happy. We're very happy. You know why?"

"Why?"

"You're going to be a big brother."

CHAPTER 10
SOMETHING'S GOTTA GIVE

L ate that night, Mark lay motionless in bed inside his dark and silent house, hearing nothing but the slow, rhythmic breathing of
his beautiful wife. It'd been several hours after news of the baby broke
and they'd made all the obligatory phone calls to friends and relatives
and of course Jennifer had wasted no time posting the news to Facebook. Elated, Mark had taken the family to their favorite restaurant,
Maggianos, where they'd had a wonderful time. In fact, it'd all happened so quickly that now was the first time Mark was able to digest
his day. He wouldn't have long to think about it though. Completely
exhausted from the night before plus hearing news of baby Stiles,
Mark had popped an Advil PM to make sure he got enough rest. He
always hated the foggy feeling the morning after, but he couldn't go
through another day like he'd just endured.

If he didn't have enough motivation before to make some changes in his life, he certainly did now! No matter what you do for a
living, babies are expensive. Insurance was going to go up, the cost

of the delivery, outfitting the guest bedroom to be a nursery. Mark smiled at this thought. The guest bedroom was usually vacant except for the times that Jennifer's parents came to visit. Mark and his in-laws got along okay, but there's only so much you can take of people you're forced to love. They would surely come visit, but now they couldn't stay in the house.

In that moment, Mark loved the baby even more.

Then the sinking feeling hit.

Oh God, are we going to have to move? The house will be a little more cramped, but it's both a blessing and a curse not to have a guest room. Our school system is fine, I guess, but with Jason starting first grade next year and the baby following him a few years after, maybe we should start looking. But what if we can't sell the house for what we want? What if we can't find anything with such limited inventory? What if . . .

The Advil kicked in and Mark's mind drifted into beautiful oblivion, taking his panicked thoughts with it.

<Bleep, Bleep>

<Bleep, Bleep>

<Bleep, Bl—

Mark grabbed his phone and slid his finger on just the right spot to prevent it from going off a third time. He lay dead still, not breathing. This was the make-or-break moment with the alarm clock. Depending on how deeply Jennifer was sleeping and how much Mark disturbed the bed trying to wake up, she might be waking up with him—something she wouldn't be happy about at all. Satisfied he hadn't wakened her, he managed to slip out of bed without stepping on Boomer's face (or a Lego) and tiptoed out of the room, shutting the door behind him.

It was 6:16 in the morning and Mark was determined to carve out a little time to read *The Miracle Morning. Time to see what all this hoopla is about.*

Funny how we act when faced with massive change. A few days ago

I wouldn't have dreamed I'd intentionally *be up this early in the morning—doing "feel-goodery nonsense" no less.*

Mark went straight for the coffee maker and flipped it on. He'd read long ago that the quickest way to form a habit was to make it easy to do and take out the slightest obstacle. While it didn't take that long to prepare coffee in the morning, it was enough of a chore to discourage him from getting up if he knew that magical liquid energy didn't await him shortly after rising. With last night's momentous occasion, he needed a few minutes to figure out where the book had wound up. He finally found it in the living room laying on top of his other business books. Jennifer must have moved it as they were leaving for dinner. Mark surveyed the books he'd collected over the years.

This collection is smaller than it should be, Mark.

There were the staples: *How to Win Friends and Influence People, Think and Grow Rich,* and *Rich Dad Poor Dad,* but there were also a few Anthony Robbins and Zig Ziglar books thrown into the mix.

Secretly, Mark admired people that achieved extraordinary results a good deal and often daydreamed about what his lifestyle would look like if he could achieve similar results.

Well, given yesterday's events, my lifestyle and career might involve cleaning out Porta Potties.

Clearing his thoughts, he moved back into the kitchen, setting the book on the table and pouring himself a cup of coffee. Finally ready, Mark sat at the table and cracked the book open. He set a timer on his phone to go off at 7:00 so that he could get to work on time.

Gosh, it's already 6:27!

He'd wasted about fifteen minutes without realizing it. Mark turned back to the book and dove into the introduction.

When Mark's alarm went off just over half-an-hour later, he was disappointed at how quickly the time had passed. Though brief, Hal's story was engrossing, and Mark couldn't believe what this man had overcome. nor the unwavering determination to succeed he possessed. During college, Hal was struck by a drunk driver in a head-on collision. It made Mark's present situation look trivial—a complete joke. *A head-on collision on the highway?!*

Mark had been rear-ended a little over six months ago at a stoplight. The sound inside the car is what had rattled him the most. He couldn't imagine being hit *head-on* driving at eighty miles per hour. Although he'd been reported dead at least once, Hal had survived the crash and miraculously managed to make a mostly full recovery. Surprisingly, Hal didn't write *The Miracle Morning* until after his *second* rock-bottom experience: an inevitable collision with The Great American Financial Crisis of 2008.

Hal lost his house, his income, and almost lost himself in depression. In the depths of his despair, a mentor and friend reached out to him and helped him fight through his circumstances by challenging Hal to take charge of his situation. As Hal began to act on the advice and took positive, meaningful steps to improve his life, he developed a few of his own rituals and methods to radically change his situation. After a short time, he discovered that he was on to something and authored *The Miracle Morning*.

Mark briefly debated lingering a little longer to start Chapter 1, but decided against it. He planned to get a jump on his day to avoid a repeat of the last few weeks that had landed him where he was now. As he headed up to the room, he fired off a quick email to Tyler.

<Tyler, I picked up the book yesterday and woke up a little earlier this morning to start it. Made it through the intro. Looking forward to Chapter 1.>

The swooshing paper airplane noise issued from his iPhone. At the top of the stairs, he looked down the hall at Jason's room and the guest bedroom next to it. It was rare that he was up before Jennifer. She usually got "her boys" out of bed, and Mark generally only had enough time in the mornings to hit the shower and say goodbye to Jason before he battled the mean streets of Dallas. Mark paused at the door of the guest bedroom and leaned against it. He imagined what this room would look like in light yellow or blue compared to the awful, awful maroon it was now. It was macabre, but it always made him think that a blood bath had taken place in rooms with dark, red walls.

Who thought that was a good idea?

After the walls were painted, the crib would go near the window so that the baby could see outside and have some natural light. The room was fairly large so they'd have no problem fitting the changing station, Pack 'n Play, and whatever other overpriced baby necessities Target offered. Target was Jennifer's obsession. They couldn't enter a Target, even just to grab something quickly, without perusing a few of the aisles.

Mark looked at the clock on his phone and knew he needed to get moving. He quietly opened Jason's door and peered inside. The room was mostly dark save for the glow-in-the-dark stars on the ceiling and a handful of nightlights Jason insisted kept the Boogieman away. A quick glance around the room confirmed that all sockets were occupied by nightlights in the form of a Lego, Batman, and several other shapes he didn't recognize.

Mark always tried to wake his son up in fun, amusing ways. Today he settled on using one of Jason's Legos. Some of the larger pieces generally had a light and sound kit to make laser or engine noises. Mark picked up a large kit and brought it to his son's bed. Kneeling down face-to-face with Jason, Mark pressed the button on the kit to make the engine start. An electronic "Vroom, vroom" issued from the kit followed by the sound of screeching tires. Startled by the noise, Jason's sleepy eyes flashed opened but closed again as he realized his dad was tormenting him. Jason groaned and tried to duck under the sheets, but Mark quickly grabbed the bedding and flung it off the bed.

"Daaaad!" Jason whined as he tried to avoid getting up.

"It's morning, Jason! Time to seize the day!" Mark responded, dancing around his son's bed. Realizing that sounds and antics weren't going to be enough, Mark grabbed Jason and swirled him around in circles. Soon, Jason was laughing and trying to push away from his dad. "Okay, okay, I'm up," Jason groaned. Satisfied, Mark playfully threw Jason back on his bed and ran out of the room.

In record time Mark showered, shaved, and was heading out the door. He and Jennifer shared a particularly long and romantic kiss at the kitchen table, which got them an exaggerated "EWWW!" from Jason. Mark tousled his son's head as he bid them farewell and strode to his car. He felt great today, and he could tell it was more from just the extra sleep he'd gotten. Even the fogginess from the Advil PM was noticeably absent. It had been a long time since he had intentionally gotten out of bed early to do something for himself, and it was definitely paying off. On the way to work, Mark mulled over what his lifestyle would look like. As he sat at a red light a few blocks from the office, a single thought broke to the surface:

Why do you want to have an abundant life?

Waiting for the light to turn, Mark played with the thought for a few moments. Why did he care if he had an abundant life? What did that accomplish for him, or his family, or better yet, the greater good? He realized he was on to something and filed the thought away for further review.

CHAPTER 11
ARGUING FOR ADVANCEMENT

Mark arrived at his office, feeling upbeat and strangely excited. He began his daily work routine and fired up his computer.

This thing always takes five minutes to boot up. I need IT to take a look at it soon.

While the computer was booting up, Mark went to the office kitchen to brew some coffee and grab some ice water. Grabbing his cup from next to the sink, Mark inspected it, thought it was good enough, and put a pod in the Keurig.

The front receptionist walked in.

"Good morning, Mary. How are you today?" Mark asked in a genuinely pleasant tone.

"I'm good, Mark. You sound like you're in a good mood this morning. Going to be a good month?"

"It'll be okay. I finally got a good night's sleep and woke up early this morning. So, it's off to a good start at least. Plus, Jennifer and I just found out we're expecting!"

Mary loved babies and squealed with delight. "Oh, Mark, that is wonderful news! I'm so happy for you guys. Please tell Jennifer 'congratulations' for me." Her demeanor then changed and she continued. "I sure hope your good mood won't be ruined this afternoon when Paul comes by." She smiled warmly, patted him on the shoulder and handed him his cup of coffee before reloading the Keurig.

Mark leaned against the counter in the kitchen and blew on his steaming mug. "Hmmm . . . was there an e-mail that Paul was coming by?"

"No, not that I saw. I think he's just making his rounds to the offices in the area. All I know is that he's got a pretty long meeting with David early this afternoon."

"Oh, okay." Mark blew more steam out of his cup. He'd met Paul a few times and he seemed like a pretty cool guy. But Paul could be rather blunt about handling a situation and didn't always gather the facts before reprimanding someone. If the company hadn't made an official announcement, this may just be a casual meeting between David and Paul, but Mark suspected there could be more.

Maybe I'm just being paranoid. I'm being self-conscious about what happened yesterday and I'm putting two-and-two together that may not equal four.

After chatting for a minute or two more about the baby, Mark gathered his things and headed back to his desk. The office was buzzing with activity: phones ringing throughout the cubicles, copiers spitting out print jobs, and co-workers laughing and talking in their cubes. As he expected, when he got back to his desk, his computer was prompting him to log on.

After he was fully logged on, Mark looked at Todd Duncan's website and considered making a reservation for the event. The home page was definitely geared toward marketing this event called Sales Mastery, "a three-day event in Desert Springs, California, that would absolutely change your life." Mark had no idea where that was, but the name probably meant it was in southwest California. Clicking through the event information, he saw numerous speakers and mortgage professionals he'd never heard of. That didn't surprise him though. The mortgage business wasn't exactly a sexy industry that caught a lot of publicity. Well, not a lot of *good* publicity anyway. The financial crisis was still fresh on America's mind.

On the registration page, Mark gulped at the event cost of $795. It wasn't as expensive as he thought it would be, but he'd need to justify the cost to Jennifer before he pulled the trigger. The upcoming baby situation would complicate this conversation, but he felt that he needed to attend this event in order to keep his promise to Tyler and to turn things around at work *and* in life.

That conversation won't be fraught with pressure now, will it Mark?

He supposed he was going to have a "come-to-Jesus meeting" (as his father would say) with her about what he was struggling with. Thinking ahead, he checked flight and hotel costs. At $300 a night, the hotel was definitely a bit spendy. He checked a few surrounding hotels and found one close by had a ninety-four-dollar-a-night special with free transportation service to surrounding areas.

Bingo. Jennifer will have to appreciate my effort there, right?

He looked at some pictures of the hotel to make sure he wouldn't end up in the missing persons section of the local paper and decided the place was good enough. It even had a comforting name: The Oasis Inn. Finally, the airfare. He'd learned from a recent news broadcast that if you are willing to travel during non-peak times, you could save a substantial amount of money. Sure enough, the first flight out of Dallas to California at 3:35 a.m. was several hundred dollars cheaper than a ticket during peak flight time. The same was true of the trip back. Mark did the math and factored in food and drinks for the few days he'd be there.

Wow, this is still going to cost about $2,000. That's not unreasonable, but it's not something I'd planned to spend so soon. Maybe I can put it *on our credit card? But I hate playing the debt game like that. I could get myself into trouble in a hurry—just like last time. And Jennifer would not appreciate that again.*

Mark mentally prepared his case with all his motivations, as well as his defense to the most likely rebuttals. Jennifer was pretty sharp and often thought of issues he hadn't. While he was adamant about going on this trip, if there was something huge he hadn't thought of, he would certainly consider postponing it. Tyler would just have to deal with it. Mark took three quick breaths and called his wife. Jennifer picked up on the second ring.

"Hey, hon. How's work going?"

"It's off to a good start. I didn't destroy my mouth on the coffee, so it's probably going to be a good day," Mark joked.

Jennifer giggled on the other end. "Well, that's good. What's up?"

"Remember when I told you I bumped into Tyler the other day? Yesterday morning, we talked about my work for a while. He saw a few issues I've been having and recommended that I attend an upcoming mortgage sales conference. He's attended before and followed the hosts' business model for several years. He insists this event and speaker are the primary drivers of his success."

There was a slight pause before Jennifer responded. "Oh . . . okay. It's a little unexpected. And the timing could certainly be better." He knew what was coming next. "What kinds of trouble have you been having at work? You haven't mentioned anything to me."

"It's probably nothing big." Mark tried to downplay the seriousness of his discussion with David. He didn't want to be dishonest, but there was no reason to add too much stress to her life right now. "I'm mostly tired of the rollercoaster of my sales career and I need to figure out how to do business better than I have been. It's just wearing me out."

"I've known something has been eating at you for a while. You've been more stressed, worked longer hours and . . ." She stopped herself but Mark knew what she was implying: the fact he kept missing

Jason's activities. She calmly continued, "I've seen it in your eyes, Mark. I appreciate the call but you don't normally run stuff like this past me. What's *really* up?"

Deploy argument #1.

"Nah, that's not true baby! We always talk about this kind of stuff. The bottom line is that I feel this conference is very important for me—for us. Especially considering our new addition. The conference is at the end of this month for three days. And, well . . . I estimate it's going to be about two thousand dollars all in."

Jennifer practically guffawed. "Two thousand dollars! Who's going to be there, the Pope? Are you serious?"

Mark smiled. "Yes."

"Well, you know I trust your judgment, but I just paid the bills this morning and it's not like we're ahead right now. Plus, we need to be saving for the baby, and even then a bad month for you or something bad happening with one of us would put us in a tough spot. Can't you push this?"

Deploy rebuttal #1.

"You're absolutely right. Now *isn't* the right time. But there hasn't been a *good time* in over twelve months! It's a bit of money up front, but if the seminar works, I'll make that money back and more. On *one* deal. It could be a real game-changer for me Jen."

"But you hate that kind of stuff! I've heard you bad mouth self-improvement over our entire relationship. Don't you think this will be a waste of money? Why will this be different?"

Deploy rebuttal #2.

This is what Mark had been worried about. Jennifer was absolutely right. This was a self-improvement event and he'd been against these gatherings for years. He had always believed himself to be strong enough to fulfill his own destiny and provide his own way.

"Yeah, you're right. That's another good point, but I came to a realization with Tyler yesterday. I'm not living the kind of life that I want."

"What? What do you mean?" Jennifer sounded hurt.

"No, no. Don't take that the wrong way. Please don't do that. You and Jason are the best part of my life. But I'm not happy right now in my work life. I didn't even realize that until twenty four hours ago. I've gotten lazy and I'm tired of living paycheck to paycheck, month to month. That's not the kind of life I want to give you and Jason and our baby. I want to work less, or take trips with you, or put Jason into Select soccer, and I don't think that we'll be able to do that on my current path. Does that make sense?"

Mark heard Jennifer's voice wavering. "Let's talk more about this when you get home. Can you wait to book the trip until then?"

Deploy final rebuttal.

"No, I really shouldn't wait. The price could go up on everything and I don't think much will change from our conversation. But I definitely do want to talk and I'll share with you more of what's been going on."

"Okay." A long pause. "Well, I love you, hon. I'll see you tonight."

"I love you too. Please know that I'm doing this for all of us."

Mark hung up the phone and sighed in relief. That went better than he had expected, and it certainly could have gone a different direction. Jennifer did make a good observation. They were tight on cash and they needed to be careful. If he could cut some costs, he definitely would.

I doubt I could get the company to pay for the conference given my current status, but maybe I can ask for reimbursement if the conference increases my numbers?

Mark took a brief break and grabbed some more coffee. He was starting to feel just the slightest bit tired from waking up earlier than normal, but he was determined to keep his energy levels up today. He was going to make it a point to be as productive as possible.

Fresh cup of Joe in hand, he settled back into his desk chair and got to work.

CHAPTER 12
THE COUNTDOWN BEGINS

Shortly after lunch, Mark heard a knock. He looked up, but couldn't tell who was outside of his frosted window. Quickly tidying up, he responded, "Come in!"

Mark was shocked to see Paul but hid his surprise. Standing, he greeted Paul with a warm smile and handshake. "Hey, good afternoon, Paul. How are you?"

"Hello, Mark." Paul smiled in return. "I'm doing well. How have things been with you?"

"Oh, they're coming along. Just trying to stay on top of the summer grind."

What looked like a forced smile flashed across Paul's face, but his eyes didn't match his mouth. "Yeah, that's good to hear. We need to make hay while the sun is shining."

"That's right, that's right. Did you drop by to talk shop for a bit?"

"Actually no. I wanted to see if you had a few minutes at four to meet with David and me in his office."

"Uh, yeah, I can meet, but it'll have to be at 4:15 at the earliest. I have a scheduled prospect call with a referral. Will that work?"

"Oh, well that certainly comes first. Let's plan on 4:15 then. If you need a few more minutes, just shoot us an e-mail."

With that, Paul smiled (but not the eyes) and stepped out of Mark's office, shutting the door lightly behind him. The smile slowly faded from Mark's face as his heart beat a little faster.

This isn't good at all. This is prime time and Paul and David want to meet with me? It must be an impromptu performance review. Or worse.

Throughout the day, Mark had seen some of his colleagues going back to David's office, but he assumed those were planned meetings. Maybe they were, but Mark was no fool. He needed to go into this meeting prepared. He'd have about an hour to pull his sales numbers and come up with a convincing pitch as to why they needed to give him just a little more time to try to right the ship. If Mark ended up just being paranoid and the past didn't come up, all the better.

Just before his prospect call, Mark finished pulling his numbers for the year and for each of the last twelve months. They could be better, but they could also be worse. Just to be proactive, he also pulled his number of resubs waiting for final approval, the average time it took to get his loan approvals, and a rough timeline of when he'd hit different milestones in the loan process. He'd need to analyze it more later, but he had a few ideas about where to start—with or without Tyler's help.

The prospect call went fairly smoothly. Mark answered the prospect's questions and felt he was building trust. He thought he was home free until the man on the other line finally popped the question.

"You know, Mark, I completely forgot to ask. What's the interest rate for the mortgage we're talking about?"

Mark was a little taken aback at the timing of the question. He almost always dealt with this question earlier in the call yet Mr. Garcia had waited until right at the end when he thought he'd completed the application.

"Uh, well it depends on several factors."

I need to work on my professional rebuttals. Way to stumble over your words to build even more confidence, Mark, you idiot.

"Your credit score, the loan program, and what the market is doing all impact the interest rate."

"Okay, that makes sense. So what does it look like right now?"

"What does your afternoon look like Mr. Garcia? I generally like to scrub all the information you've provided so that I can make sure I didn't miss anything. That better prepares me to put together a comprehensive fee and interest rate schedule so you can see what the entire picture looks like."

"Okay, that sounds good. I'd definitely like to see all that before we move forward. I'm free any time this afternoon, so just call when you can."

"Okay, it may be close to five, but I'll give you a call."

Mark hung up the phone, not nearly as pumped as he was thirty seconds ago. It's not that he didn't like having the inevitable rate and fee conversation, but it had certainly caught him off guard. That one question was one of the few things that could derail an otherwise successful connection—like when you have a fish on the line and you've just about got it to shore when it suddenly changes direction and jumps out of the water, breaking the line. Sometimes borrowers had unreasonable expectations of what they should pay, and some-times Mark's rates were just flat out higher than a competitor's. He never really felt like he controlled that conversation. Mark just hoped he could build enough of a connection to overcome any objections.

Glancing at the clock, Mark found he had a few minutes before meeting with Paul and David. He intended to take advantage of ev-ery single one of them. On a whim, Mark printed the receipt to the Todd Duncan Sales Mastery event. He wasn't sure what to expect in this meeting, but anything that could earn favor couldn't hurt. May-be they'd even offer to pick up the tab.

One minute to 4:15, Mark headed to the meeting, folder in hand. He took deep, slow breaths on the short walk to David's office. He was nervous and he sure as hell didn't want that to show in his voice. That would practically be an admission of guilt. Mark raised his knuckles and rapped them on the door a few times. Through the frosted window, he saw a figure stand. Paul's face appeared again and he ushered Mark into the room. Greetings were exchanged and Mark took a seat at the small meeting table. Clearing his voice, Paul started the meeting.

"Mark, I know this may be a bit of a surprise, but do you know why we're having this meeting?"

"I'm not a hundred percent sure, but I'm assuming it has something to do with the meeting that I had with David yesterday. Is that right?"

"Yes, it is. I came here for an impromptu review with David and a few members of his team. The team as a whole is performing well, and you're certainly contributing to that, but this company doesn't define success merely by the volume that you're able to close. Over the last few months, I've seen some of the metrics that we track actually *decline*."

Marcus let the last word hang. Mark didn't take the bait.

"Digging into the data, you and a few others popped up on to our radar and we need to address the underlying problems. This meeting will serve as your sixty-day notice that things either need to turn around with your numbers or we need to part ways."

Mark felt like cold water had just been poured down his spine. Trying not to show the shock and confusing irritation he was feeling, Mark shot a look at David, who was passively staring at some papers in front of him. David glanced up at him and then looked at Paul. "Paul, do you want to elaborate on some of the numbers that you were referring to?"

"Yes, I think that'd be helpful. Don't you, Mark?"

Mark nodded in agreement and remembered the folder in his lap. "I brought my numbers as well. I reviewed a few of the metrics earlier, but what exactly are you looking to be more in line?"

"Good question. Without a doubt, your volume is in line with what we're looking for. Sure, we'd love for all LO's to be hitting ten-plus units a month, but not everyone wants to do that, and frankly not everyone *can* do that. What I'm most concerned with, however, is the strain that your production puts on the system."

Mark wanted to argue his case but remained silent.

"From our calculations, your average processor submissions are three-point-five and your underwriter touches are nearly three-point-five on average. Additionally, the number of conditions that your files receive are about one-and-a-half times higher than the average file. We've looked at your borrower base and the data does not support a complicated scenario with more conditions.

Mark sighed. Paul didn't stop.

"Finally, we spoke with your processors and underwriters because the initial data reflects poorly on them. After reviewing this data with them, we discovered that they regularly receive requests to rush your files along and push conditions through to funding, all resulting in errors and fire drills. Maybe the worst part of all of this is that it's putting your fellow originators in a bad spot. When they do a good job, their files are delayed because your processor and underwriter are having to spend extra time on yours while still trying their very best to handle files fairly on a first-come, first-served basis."

Mark rose from his seat, cold water turning to steam. "Those numbers seem inflated. What I pulled is not nearly as negative. Here, look at th—"

"Mark, let me stop you right there. I appreciate that you came to this meeting prepared, but the metrics that we keep at the home office are rock solid. We've tested them over and over again and they're *always* accurate. What you pulled may not include all of the information because you don't have the same access to internal data. The question really is, what are you going to do to turn the ship around? We value all of our originators, and you've been with us for some time. We don't want to fire you, but we're not going to tolerate these issues any longer."

"I don't understand why I'm being put on a sixty-day notice. I didn't even get a formal warning until yesterday!"

"We disagree," Paul calmly replied, staring steadily into Mark's eyes. "David has mentioned to you numerous times that your metrics were out of whack. Isn't that right, David?"

"That's right."

Mark sat back down and ran his fingers through his hair, an old habit that surfaced when he needed to think. Tight-lipped, he stared at Paul and David, struggling for the right words to rectify his position. He remembered the receipt for the Sales Mastery conference and his conversations with Tyler. Leaning forward, Mark found the receipt and put it on the table.

"I'll be attending the Todd Duncan Sales Mastery conference at the end of this month. I've already paid for the event."

"Hmm." Paul picked up the receipt, glanced at it, then handed it back to Mark. "I'm familiar with Todd Duncan, but your volume isn't a problem Mark. How is this conference going to help with your quality issues?"

"My mentor"—*Gosh that sounds weird*—"believes that some of the issues I'm having right now are stemming from a poor execution strategy on the sales end. He highly recommended this conference, in addition to a few other things."

"I see," Paul replied. "Do you expect the company to pay for this?"

"No, I'm doing this on my own. For my career."

"Given where we are at right now, the company won't pay for this, but if you're able to turn things around, we'll reimburse you for your event and travel expenses." David shot Paul a questioning look, clearly not expecting this. Paul held up a hand to keep a debate from forming. "I'm interested that you have a mentor. How long has this been going on? Is it someone that we would know?"

Mark relaxed. The conversation seemed to be changing for the better. "It's actually an old colleague of mine who's also in the mortgage business but is far more successful than I am. I ran into him at a networking event and what started as a casual conversation turned into a mentoring relationship. We've just started meeting, so I'm not sure what to expect."

Paul nodded, watching Mark intently. Mark kept his gaze. "Well Mark, I have to tell you I'm pleasantly surprised. Of everyone we've talked to today, you are certainly the most proactive. Unfortunately, this doesn't change our sixty-day timeline, but if nothing else, I appreciate your commitment to improve and you have a head start. You and David will continue to have regular meetings to monitor progress and he'll loop me in as needed. Sound like a plan?"

What a condescending little . . . I'm a grown man, Paul! I'm a grown man, David! I don't even like or respect either of you all that much!

Mark managed a yes and the meeting was over. He shook hands with both men and exited. Apparently the office had gotten the memo that something was going on in David's office. Several heads were turned his way to see how the meeting had ended. Mark tried to mask his emotions but didn't think he was doing a good job. As he walked past cubicles and open offices, he heard muffled whispers and uncomfortably locked eyes with several others. They were all studying his face, trying to make sense of the meeting. Did he get fired, or did he get a pat on the back and an "attaboy"?

Back in his office, Mark shut the door and slumped into his chair. Thank God he'd registered for that event. The outcome probably wouldn't have been any different, but he certainly looked better in the eyes of management. He wasn't a complete waste of their time. Mark was surprised to see that the meeting had lasted twenty minutes. It'd felt much shorter.

I guess time flies when you're in front of the firing squad.

He needed to put together Mr. Garcia's fee and rate schedule and call him back, but just didn't feel like it now. He leaned his head back on the chair and for a fleeting moment, Mortgage Mark briefly considered blowing it off. He came up with several bogus excuses for why he should just leave early and go grab a beer, the strongest being that he deserved it after the brutal meeting he'd just endured. But on the other hand, he knew his production for the next month was down. He couldn't afford to be weak and lazy now.

Dig deep. Hal talks about doing the things you don't want to do when you know you should. This is how you change.

Over the years, Mark had developed several tools that were invaluable to him. After reviewing the file for a few minutes, he plugged the numbers into the spreadsheet and it spit out a bottom-line cash-to-closing amount. The rate was probably higher than Mr. Garcia wanted. Mark knew if he absolutely had to he could probably get an approval to lower the rate, but that likely wouldn't go over well. Mark dialed Mr. Garcia and was grateful when he picked up. He never wanted to send something like this to a prospect without having them on the phone first. The quickest way to overcome objections was in real time, not when a prospect had opportunity to stew on something they may not understand.

"Mr. Garcia, it's Mark Stiles. Did I catch you at a good time?"

"Sure Mark, I was expecting your call."

"Great, are you near a computer?" It took about ten minutes to go over the document, but by the end Mark had gotten a verbal commitment from Mr. Garcia to proceed. Mark would send out the disclosures tomorrow and request the required paperwork then. He was anxious to get home and share with Jennifer what had transpired over the last few days.

He would conveniently forget to share about his sixty-days notice.

I wouldn't even be granted time for rebuttals to that.

CHAPTER 13
FALLING FOR THE FEEL-GOODERY
56 DAYS

<B leep, Bleep>
<Bleep, Bleep>
<Bleep, Bl—

Mark had forgotten to turn the alarm volume down the night before so as he frantically tried to shut his phone off, Jennifer stirred and gruffly whispered, "What TIME is it?"

Mark rubbed her back gently and replied, "It's 5:30. Go back to bed, kiddo."

Jennifer grumbled an unintelligible response—probably something about him being a crazy bastard—and buried her head under her pillow.

Even on a Saturday, Mark was determined to keep the streak he had going with his Miracle Morning. Every morning that week, he'd woken up earlier and earlier to gradually adjust his body to the new sleep schedule. It seemed to be working, although this morning he felt more tired than he had any other morning that week, likely a combination of consistently waking up early, stress, and it being Saturday.

Mark padded down the stairs and was greeted with the soothing smell of Starbucks, fresh and hot in the coffee pot. By day three, he'd finally started preparing the coffee the night before and was glad he had. It made getting up easier, and he was able to dive in sooner. Maybe in time he could drop the coffee. It definitely made the physical portion less enjoyable. He always got to enjoy the coffee a second time around, one way or another.

Mark had devoured *The Miracle Morning* over the last few days and had committed to memory what Hal Elrod called his SAVERS routine: scribing, affirmations, visualizations, exercise, reading, and silence or meditation. He certainly hadn't mastered them. By far, the ten minutes of silence was the hardest thing for him to focus on.

There's clearly a reason why the majority of the population does not spend time meditating.

During the ten minutes of silence, Mark couldn't keep his mind from drifting and thinking about work or how his fantasy sport team was going to do this week. He also found himself thinking about Jason or the new baby. But he was trying nonetheless. Focusing throughout the day seemed to be getting easier, a byproduct he attributed to his morning meditation.

Without a doubt, the thing he enjoyed most was the writing. At first, it had felt strange and forced, but he was starting to find his voice. It was actually cathartic. He would write about his frustrations mostly, but he was trying to pepper in some goals and what he was going to try to accomplish during the upcoming day. During this time, he focused on the thought that came to him after starting his Miracle Morning: *why do I care about changing my circumstances?*

Mark wasn't sure, but he thought if he could answer this fundamental question it would help unlock the drive he needed. In addition to this central question, he also tried to answer other important questions like: why do I originate loans? What does it provide to me and my family? How can I use success in business to fulfill me? Slowly but surely he felt himself getting closer to those answers.

Yesterday, he'd actually done something that was on his list of goals that he didn't even realize he'd knocked out until the drive home. It was as if writing down the goal had forced him to do it subconsciously. Mark was beginning to understand why this was so appealing to Tyler and how much could be accomplished if he could remain dedicated.

Not that I'd tell Tyler that.

Dedication. That's what he was worried about right now. He'd been on fire for this morning routine, but as the days wore on and life got in the way, would he be able to keep it up?

Mark knew he had an obsessive personality. He would pick up new things quickly, but his passion was intense and short-lived, like pouring a can of gasoline on a fire instead of allowing a slow burn with a thick log. The clearest example of this was a few years ago when he'd trained for six months straight for a Tough Mudder race. He'd shed stubborn fat, gained muscle, and was arguably in the best shape of his life. The day after the race, he stopped going to the gym altogether. All motivation was gone after he'd accomplished his goal. His body now was a shadow of its former self—something he was going to work on in the exercise section of his mornings.

Mark had confirmed with Tyler the day before that they would have their catch-up call this morning at 6:30. He needed to get a move on if he wanted to fit it all in before the call. For his reading, Mark began *The 7 Habits of Highly Effective People*. He wasn't very far along, but he knew he was going to like the book. At 6:30, he received a text message from Tyler with one word: Ready?

Mark responded and a moment later his phone chirped in his hand.

"Mornin' Tyler," Mark said as he cleared his throat.

"Good Miracle Morning, Mark! It sounds like you've been making some progress with the book?"

"Yeah, actually I have. I finished the book yesterday and I've been focusing on getting up a little earlier each morning so that I can devote enough time to do each one right."

"Wow, that's great. I honestly didn't expect you to embrace the Miracle Morning so quickly. Why do you think you did?"

"Well, I received two very important but opposite-ends-of-the-spectrum announcements this week. First, I found out that I'm going to have another baby."

"What?! That's excellent, Mark. Congratulations, bud!"

"Thanks! We're very excited. Our son, Jason, is also happy. We're not sure what the sex is, but I'll let you know when we do."

"Yeah, do that."

Mark plowed ahead. "The other announcement was that I have, or had, sixty days to turn things around at work or I can find another mortgage bank to originate loans at."

There was silence on the other line. "Are you still there Tyler?"

"Yeah, sorry. I was just a little shocked by the two extremes of the news. I take it the sixty-day notice was a surprise?"

"Completely. I hadn't realized the magnitude of my problem until the same week we started talking, and then the wheels just came off. I'm putting all of my eggs in this Miracle Morning and Todd Duncan basket. I hope they pan out."

"Well, it's not a silver bullet, but you've proven to me so far that you're serious about making some positive changes in your life. I've gotten burned a few times investing in other people's lives that don't have any willpower or ambition and it's just a waste of my time. I think you'll be different though."

"Thanks." It was a bit awkward, but how else could he respond?

"Let's talk a little about the Todd Duncan conference. As I mentioned, none of this is a guarantee that it's going to change things for you, but you mentioned to me the other day that you didn't feel like you had the motivation that you used to with this business. Is that still true?"

"It is. Some days I feel like I have to force myself to get up and go to work. That may be because I'm terrified of the fires that I'm going to face, but I can tell I don't have that same drive to go out and sell and educate."

"Sales Mastery will definitely help with that then. It's not as intensive as Todd's High Trust Sales Academy, but you'll pick up some valuable selling tools and techniques. One of the primary benefits of attending Sales Mastery is that it will recharge your mortgage sales battery and provide you with insight as to what is possible in this business. It's all about ordinary people who executed a specific strategy that paid off big."

"Well, this thing is costing me an arm and a leg. I better be able to close a few extra deals when I come back."

"Just go with an open mind. Most years, the first session or two will be all about finding your purpose. Getting your fire back. I suspect that will be hugely beneficial for you. Take a ton of notes and just work on coming back with a few strategies that you like and can execute."

They continued to talk about their respective Miracle Mornings for the next twenty minutes. When they hung up, they'd scheduled a face-to-face meeting at Tyler's office after the conference to debrief and for Tyler to explain some of his techniques for closing loans on time with fewer problems.

As Mark headed upstairs to wake Jennifer up, he chuckled.

Something's gotta give, or I'm getting into real estate.

CHAPTER 14
SALES MASTERY DAY ONE
48 DAYS

Mark walked into the grand conference room, dumbfounded by the size and scope of the program. He'd read about the event online, but nothing had prepared him for this. This wasn't just a single large ballroom, it was three large ballrooms connected together to make one massive meeting room. He couldn't be sure, but the room must have had between 1,200 and 1,500 chairs. In the background, the latest Red Hot Chili Peppers track was blasting and several beach balls were being tossed around the room as a carousel of different-colored lights danced across the back wall and ceiling.

It's a giant party. Can mortgages really be fun again?

Motivational quotes from Todd's books slid across the main projectors along with a countdown. Mark reluctantly felt himself drawn into the energy.

This is how they hook you with the hype.

He was early so he sat in the middle of the room near the aisle.

Over the next hour, the entire room filled and pulsed with anticipation. Mark hadn't seen something like this since college, sitting in the school stadium, surrounded by thousands of fans. The murmurs of the crowd turned into a unified chant. The room was electric and buzzing with excitement. Everyone around Mark began counting down in unison, following the final ticks of the clock on the screen.

"Ten! Nine! Eight!"

They all began to stand, and Mark followed suit.

"Seven! Six! Five!"

The crowd began to shout at the top of their lungs.

What is this? New Year's Eve?

"Four! Three! Two! O—"

The final number was lost in the sound of overwhelming applause.

Todd Duncan had appeared.

Mark guessed Todd was in his early fifties but had the energy of a much younger man. Todd greeted people at the front of the room while laughing, clapping, and keeping the energy up. He gave a thumbs-up to someone at the back of the room, and the music faded as his microphone went live.

"Good evening, everyone! I'm so excited that you're here for the annual Sales Mastery Conference!" The crowd erupted again. "Go ahead and take your seats and let's get started. We've got a lot to cover over the next few days and I know that you're going to take away massive, massive value."

A few isolated "Whoops!" rang out.

"As you all know, I've been hosting these conferences for over fifteen years because I know that my mission—my purpose in life—is to help you as a loan officer succeed and excel at the highest level. I learned early on in my career that only certain activities truly provided me success, so I made sure that I doubled down on those activities. I stopped doing what other loan officers were doing that was getting them nowhere."

Is he looking directly at me?

"By the time I stopped originating, I'd built a business of over one billion dollars in closed volume. I'd achieved what I considered a great deal of success, but one issue I struggled with was my purpose in life. As my success grew, so did my deep-seated desires to fill a void in my life. I've only said this a few times, but I struggled with drugs at one point in an effort to fill that void."

Mark was completely taken aback with Todd's opening story. This man had really originated that much volume? He'd struggled with drugs and now he was hosting this type of seminar?

What am I doing with my life?

Mark got lost in the rest of the story as he wrestled with his own thoughts. A few minutes later, he was interrupted by people around him grabbing something under their chairs. He tuned back in to what Todd was saying.

"Like I said, I don't normally do this exercise at Sales Mastery. This is something that's typically done on the first night of Sales Academy, which is a significantly smaller group, however, as I was putting together this year's program, I felt drawn to go through this exercise and share this with you. I didn't want to keep such a phenomenal exercise from my Sales Mastery following, so if you haven't already, go ahead and get the binder that's under your chair and turn to the first section. We're going to spend a little time working on this together in silence and then we'll share a bit as a group."

Mark leaned down and fetched his own binder, a plain three-ring white binder emblazoned with the Sales Mastery logo. Mark opened the binder and flipped to the section Todd had mentioned: "First Things First." It spanned nearly twenty pages. Mark didn't feel particularly motivated to begin pouring out his life's story. The first question asked, "Why did you become a loan officer?"

Interesting. I've been asking myself this same question over the last few weeks.

He looked up and scanned the room to see what everyone else was doing. Like him, a few people seemed lost, but most everyone had their heads down and were furiously scribbling into their binders. Mark looked at the stage as Todd scanned the crowd. Their eyes met briefly, but Todd was still sweeping the room. A determined silence had fallen.

Todd eased into the quiet like a well-rehearsed professional. "I see most of you are writing very diligently and taking this exercise seriously. A few of you aren't—"

Did he just look at me again?

"—and I hope that you will take this weekend seriously as an opportunity to radically change your life. Matters of the heart are serious. It's serious if you want to live your dreams. It's serious as to whether or not you achieve what you set out to do. Your life depends on it, and I would suspect that you have loved ones that depend on you to provide for them. By a show of hands, who's been to Sales Mastery before?"

At least ninety percent of the hands in the room shot up, maybe more.

They've spent that much multiple *times!?*

Todd continued his poll, smiling. "That's really great! Who's been at least three years?"

Some hands came down, but a huge portion of the room still looked like a human wheat field.

"And how about five?"

More hands came down. Maybe fifteen percent of the room still hand their hands up.

"How about this: who's been to my program for ten years running or more?" The next wave came down. Ten hands were left.

"That's really great. Look at that dedication! Let me ask this: has it been worth it?"

The remaining devotees nodded their heads enthusiastically and shouted yes in scary unison.

"I'll tell you what. We're on the honor system here, but I want to give all of you my new book that just came out—for free. If you've got a copy, great, you can re-gift it, but I want you to have this because I think it's going to be really meaningful to you guys. Can I get a handful of attendants to meet with the folks that still have their hands in the air? I'd like to get some of their information. Everyone else, we've got about twenty minutes left in this section before we talk about what you wrote. Spend some time diving into yourself and peeling back the layers of doubt, frustration, and regret that have been piling on you over the years. Figure out what's meaningful to you."

Well, now I feel like a jerk just sitting here and wasting valuable time. These people have come for over a decade and I bet they've filled up several sheets by now. Come on, Mark. Get in the game!.

Turning back to his binder, Mark wrote about why he first became a loan officer. Maybe it was shallow or petty, but the primary reason was for the money. He'd been at a steady job for a few years that clearly had zero upside potential because of the management structure. He'd run into an LO at a mutual friend's party and all the guy had talked about all night was how much money he was making that month alone. His monthly pay was seventy-five percent of Mark's *annual* salary at the time. Mark immediately called bull and asked to see his friend's pay stub. That was reason enough for Mark to put in his two-week notice and throw himself into the industry. Once he was in, he was hooked on providing his clients with top notch service and educating them about how best to handle their mortgages.

Presently, something bubbled to the surface of his mind: *I really started to hit my LO stride when I offered classes to real estate offices and apartment complexes.*

He'd created those seminars to educate the audience about a variety of topics, but in all honesty, he would have to admit to an ulterior motive too: the seminars had positioned him as *the* mortgage expert in their minds. His accounting background had provided him with a unique perspective within the industry. He had complemented that knowledge by learning every aspect of the origination process. From credit reports to program qualifications, Mark could recite them from heart.

But then something happened. He'd lost sight of his basic desire to educate. Instead of yearning to help, he developed an ever-growing desire to make more money any way he could. Slowly but surely, educating others had slipped away in favor of the quick-and-easy sell. He'd quit planting a future crop of originations in favor of a hunt-and-kill philosophy.

No wonder I'm on the brink of starvation at work. But at least I have an inkling of how I got to where I am now.

Encouraged by this glimmer of self-analysis, Mark moved to the second question: "What fulfillment have you gotten from being a loan officer?"

Mark almost wrote, "None," but he sat for a minute, trying to board his last train of thought. Finally, the thought pulled in to the station: *I felt the most fulfilled when I was selflessly educating others and acting as an expert in their best interests.*

Sure, the money was fulfilling, but look where that alone had gotten him the last few years? Burnt out and doing a poor job. And sitting on a sixty-day watch list.

"If you weren't originating loans, what would you be doing right now?"

What the heck would I be doing right now? Certainly not accounting. Guess I could wait forty-eight days and find out!

He scratched the stubble of the beard he was trying to grow then stroked the back of his head. It was neurotic, but it helped him think. Mark considered his life at the accounting job he'd left to enter the mortgage business. He supposed he'd be driving about the same caliber of car, but not living in quite as nice a house. They could still be renting. The income trajectory of his accounting job was relatively limited unless he was willing to make jumps between firms and specialize in a particular field. But he didn't particularly enjoy that work and was getting the sense Todd was trying to get him to think about what he would do that he would find fulfilling.

As he mulled the question, he couldn't imagine being in anything *but* real estate. Sure, he did mortgages, but they were loans on homes. The volume of each unit was fairly substantial, which meant that his cut of each sale was meaningful.

But it's only meaningful if it doesn't cause me to have a rage stroke each month.

The juices were flowing for Mark now. Somehow his thoughts were finally harmonizing and the thought struck him without warning: *I'd be a professor.*

CHAPTER 15
JUST ASK "IF..."
48 DAYS

The thought came out of left field, but it felt so right. *A professor.* He had just written about how fulfilling it had been early in his career to educate his referral partners, prospects, and clients. Heck, in college he'd even taught a supplementary economics and accounting course to help pay the bills, and he'd enjoyed that immensely.

"If you could achieve massive success in your sales career, what would that mean to you? What would you be able to accomplish with massive success?"

He reread the question a few more times.

Why have I never taken the time to stop and ask myself these questions? Oh, right, I'm a fireman in a loan officer's suit.

For the longest time, especially during the downturn, he felt successful if he could bring home enough money to keep them afloat. As the economy improved, their lives had improved too, but Mark realized it had happened almost in spite of himself and what he was actually doing. He just happened to be a net catching whatever swam into it.

What would massive success look like?

He supposed success looked like three hundred units a year, or somewhere between forty million and sixty million dollars in volume. But was that *his* definition of success or just what he had been most recently exposed to? Mark decided that he liked fifty million in volume.

Now, what would that revenue actually bring home?

Mark's math and accounting background kicked in.

Let's say I keep my personal production margin at 150 basis points. At fifty million dollars in total volume per year, that would make me roughly . . . $750,000 per year gross. $750,000 per year gross? Three quarters of a million dollars?!

Mark tried to punch holes in his logic. Surely his company, or any company for that matter, wouldn't let him keep 150 bps at that level of production. He'd have to accept a little less in order to achieve the business. So . . . maybe 125 bps was more appropriate. Even then, that would make him $625,000. Mark vaguely remembered doing this kind of math as almost a game, but now he realized that some people were achieving this or at least something similar. Hell, even if he only made $500,000 gross, that was one hell of a good living. Especially considering that slinging mortgages wasn't exactly rocket science.

Yeah, well why have you been struggling so much?

The thought punched a hole right in his fun bubble.

Maybe I need a team. Surely at that production you'd have to pay a few people to help you. They could take the roles that I don't particularly like doing, like gathering documents or chasing down minuscule conditions.

Mark decided that $500,000 in gross income would be massive success for him.

OK, so I make a half a mil . . . what would I do with all that money?

Being debt-free was the first thing that popped into his mind, but that was a relatively simple goal if he could earn that much per year.

If I could make half-a-million dollars a year, what could I do?

Mark daydreamed about family trips. The schools and sports he could put his kids into. The clothes and doodads Jennifer could get. He could finally give her all the things he'd hoped to one day provide but hadn't been able to thus far. Mark's daydream was still in full swing when Todd came back on stage, ready to get back to the program. There were still several other questions in the binder that Mark made a mental note to get back to later, particularly one about what massive success would mean to him and why that was important.

"How was that folks? Did that challenge your thinking? Did you come up with some amazing futures?" The crowd cheered and Todd smiled. "Good, good! I know I've only been able to achieve the things I want in life by having very clear answers to those types of questions. Remember folks, if you're not living for something, if you're just making it by moving from day to day, you're already dead."

Todd made a gun with his fingers and shot at Mark.

"You're just flesh and bones aimlessly walking on this earth, one foot already in your death bed. Think about the impact you want to leave on your family and communities. Think about the person you want to be remembered as and start becoming that person today. You really don't have any excuses. You don't have a single excuse for not being the best possible human being, father, husband, wife, mother, son, daughter, or loan officer you can possibly be. You owe it to your clients. You owe it to your loved ones. But most importantly, you owe it to yourself. You have to hold yourself to the highest standards possible and not allow yourself to skate by just because you can. That's cowardly, and you're ruining your life."

Todd paused. The crowd was pregnant with conviction, and Mark felt its crushing force.

What the hell have I been doing for the last few years? Why haven't I really pushed myself? Why have I held on to this negative belief that positive thinking, goal-setting, and the whole kit and caboodle was foolish? Now I feel foolish.

Todd clapped his hands. "Okay, I don't want to put a downer on the evening, but I want that to drive you to be as alert as you can be and participate as fully as possible over the next few days. I know at Sales Academy attendees have big breakthroughs during this time. Did anyone have a breakthrough just now that you want to share? Tom, can we get those mics to the front and get some runners?"

From the back of the room, a few young college-looking kids in Todd Duncan gear jogged to the front with mics, ready to meet people in the crowd to allow them a chance to speak. *Like an old Southern Baptist revival.* A woman toward the middle of the room stood up. The nearest Duncan assistant jogged over. The woman looked a little nervous, but Mark could tell she was excited to share.

"Whoo, this is a hot mic." The woman pulled it slightly away from her mouth and her face turned a shade of red.

"Hey everyone, my name is Naomi and this is my first time to attend. I came here not knowing what to expect, but knowing that I needed to do something about my career. I've always had a passion for dogs, so this year I want to double my production so that I can open a not-for-profit St. Bernard rescue in my hometown. I've always wanted to give back to the dogs I love most, and the only way I know to do that is to hit a home run this year with my origination volume!"

The crowd clapped and the people around her supportively patted her on the back.

"That's great, Naomi! Thank you for sharing! I hope you enjoy the rest of your first event. There's more great stuff to come!"

More people shared their breakthroughs. Some were more meaningful than others, but Mark could tell he wasn't alone. Most of these people had never really taken time to sit down and figure out what made them tick and what they really wanted to accomplish with their mortgage careers. It was a very tough question, one that Mark intended to spend some time during his Miracle Morning the next day to figure it out.

"So let's talk now about goals and your vision for your life. You need to create a routine that you can stick to and be consistent with."

This sounds familiar. Maybe I'm supposed to be getting a clue by now.

"If you're not constantly tracking your goals, how can you possibly stay on track to live the life you want to live? One thing I use to stay on track is a vision board."

Todd gestured to the screens on either side of him. A whiteboard filled with pictures and words appeared. Across the top of the whiteboard read "Todd's Vision Board," and it was separated by various categories: spirituality, success, happiness, and marriage.

Todd studied the audience for a moment before continuing. "All of the greats attribute some of their success in part to a vision board: a representation of everything they want out of life that's in their face and tangible every single day. I want you guys to be thinking about your own vision board and what you want to put on there. The vision board should align with your short-term and long-term goals."

Todd spaced his thumb and forefinger a few inches apart, then widened his arms out as far as they would go. The crowd laughed.

"I mentioned earlier that your goals define your life. Review them constantly and modify them as necessary. Shoot for the stars! You are only letting yourself down by not trying to be the best possible person you can be. I'm curious, by a show of hands, how many people wrote down goals this year?"

Across the room, about three-fourths raised their hands.

"Hmm, that's more than I expected. Are you guys trying to look good to your neighbors?"

A light chuckle broke out.

"Okay, moving a step further, how many of you routinely, purposefully, review the goals you wrote down at the start of the year?"

Whether by honesty or actuality, a large majority of hands went down. Maybe ten percent were left.

"That's a bit more of what I was expecting, statistically speaking. For those of you who are left, are you on track for your goals? Are you better off now than you would be otherwise?"

Everyone with a hand in the air nodded.

"See, guys? This is what I'm talking about. Your peers stand out above the rest because they're actively engaged in their own success. They treat their goals seriously, and the time they spend on them reflects that. You've gotta get serious about your life. You've gotta get serious about your own success. So where do we start? Depending on the activity, you should be able to measure a goal, whether short-term or long-term, on a weekly basis. If you wait too long to measure the success, you won't be able to change course until it's too late. So, tonight, for homework, I want you to figure out what your goals are for the next month, next six months, next year, next three years, and next five years. Will you take ownership of your life?"

Convicted and convinced, Mark nodded in scary unison with the crowd.

CHAPTER 16
A MIRACLE MORNING
47 DAYS

<B leep><Bleep> <Bleep><Ble—

Mark hit his alarm immediately. He didn't need much of a nudge to wake up this morning, despite it being 3:30 a.m. in California. He wanted to stay with Texas time, with home, and with his new schedule. He awoke ready to do business with himself. The previous day's events had left him energized. He didn't even want to go to sleep last night but made himself go to bed on time so he could stick to his Miracle Morning routine without compromise.

Mark walked over to the coffeemaker in his room and hit the power button. He'd gotten in the habit of making sure everything was ready in the morning so he wouldn't have an excuse for not doing his routine. Even his running clothes were set out on the armchair beside the bed. Like Todd had said yesterday, it *was* serious whether or not he could achieve his goals and change his life. Mark felt as if he'd spent the last few years in a complete fog and operating on limited oxygen. With Tyler introducing him to the Miracle Morning and Todd Duncan, it was like an oxygen mask firmly fitted over his nose. He felt alive.

Sitting down at the desk, Mark flipped on a lamp and opened his journal to the latest entry. As he read through entries, he was amazed at how much his thinking and writing had changed in just a short time. He realized how important this journal would be to his total development as he tracked thoughts, set goals, and reviewed how things had been going for him. Mark really wanted to dive into the remaining questions of the Sales Mastery binder. Today, he'd spend as much time as necessary to get clarity about what was important to him and why he wanted to achieve his goals.

After an hour, Mark laid his pen down and massaged his aching hand. He'd written as fast as he could, his thoughts pouring out of his mind and onto the paper like a steady stream of water. He still didn't have full clarity, but he was unpacking issues, questions, uncertainty, and opportunities like never before. Mark wondered how long it would take for him to have his full breakthrough.

Over the course of an hour, Mark uncovered his need for public recognition as being a primary need over monetary gain. Making the money he wanted to make was important, but oddly enough, it was second to his desire to have his name known. More than name recognition, it was the desire to be known as a top professional in his field for quality, volume, and expertise. Countless publications came out in Dallas each year, chiefly *D Magazine*, and oh how he wanted to be on their list next year! Beyond that, maybe he'd write a book about his journey, detailing how to be successful in the mortgage industry. A beginner's guide of sorts. Thoughts of creating an abundant life seemed somewhat juvenile at this point. Previously, Mark didn't have a single clue what an abundant life would look like, outside of what was portrayed in movies. But now, after hours of introspection, he realized that an abundant life was nothing more than a physical representation of the success he wanted to achieve. Mark felt he had something concrete now—both short-term and long-term goals.

Moving on from scribing, Mark spent twenty minutes reading Stephen Covey's *The 7 Habits of Highly Effective People*. He was just getting into the time and urgency matrix when the timer went off, indicating time to move to the next SAVERS routine.

The time and urgency matrix is such a basic concept! How have I been making it by in life without these ideas? How much more productive could I have been over the last few years if I'd divided my day into the four quadrants Stephen recommended? Instead of constantly living in the quadrant of time-sensitive emergencies, I should be focusing on less time-sensitive, but massively important endeavors, like refining my origination process to improve my numbers. And taking a different, better approach to making new relationships with realtors. And, well, this list could never end.

Next, he moved to a bit of yoga for exercise, then visualizations and affirmations, and finally silence. He was getting a little bit better at the last of the SAVERS disciplines but felt like progress was slowest with silence.

Maybe I need to do a deep dive with silence and meditation so that I can actually develop some sort of mastery.

Mark was cognizant enough to know that any time he felt hesitant to do something, it was probably the one thing he needed to focus on. After his Miracle Morning, Mark hit the showers and made it downstairs in time for breakfast. He was fascinated by the conversations at the table. He was surprised to find that several other attendees were in the same boat he was and just treading water. There were a few heavy hitters, one person having been to the Sales Mastery conference for ten years straight. If Mark could successfully implement what he learned here and through Miracle Morning, he vowed to return.

Finally, the masses headed back to the ballroom. Mark had exchanged business cards with the people nearest to him and he had been asked to sit with their group of four. He was happy to join them. Mark always prided himself on being independent, but was feeling a bit vulnerable with everything that had happened over the last few weeks. It felt good to be a part of a group.

With a fresh round of tracks playing over the speakers, the five of them navigated to the middle of the room where Mark scored an aisle seat. The digital counter appeared on the projectors again, counting down the five minutes until opening. The crowd passed the time by talking, batting beach balls around, and catching up on e-mail. Mark was grateful that today was the only weekday of the event. It always stressed him out to be away from work, unable to answer questions or unexpected issues as they arose. As the counter ran down, the crowd loudly welcomed the final seconds.

"Three! Two! One!"

CHAPTER 17
SALES MASTERY DAY TWO
47 DAYS

On cue, Todd Duncan walked onto the stage from the back curtains and clapped his hands, smiling all the while. Mark marveled at how much energy Todd sparked into the crowd and became charged up by the crowd in return—a perfect closed system. Todd motioned for the crowd to take a seat and the room quieted.

"So, everyone, did you spend some time last night and this morning getting clear on your goals?"

The crowd responded, but not nearly as intensely as Todd wanted.

"Come on, guys, wake up! We've got a full day ahead! Now, did you make a decision to get serious about changing your life or not?"

The crowd responded unanimously with a loud, resounding "yes!" Todd was satisfied.

"Okay, great. So, if you've been here before, you know this is where the fun starts. Each year, we take this time to hear from some of the top originators in the country to learn how they got to their current level of success. Again, the purpose of last night was to help you find the direction and drive that you need from within. Now, you'll learn external tools and tips you can implement into your own business immediately to dramatically increase your income potential."

At this, a few people in the crowd clapped and hollered.

"Well, I can see some of you are ready! My hope is that you all walk away from this event truly changed. But here's the sad part . . . and something that I want you to internalize."

Todd paced and his mood noticeably shifted.

"Statistically, only five percent of you are going to actually take this material and implement what you learn. Five percent! How can so few people be driven to change their lives and the lives of those they love? Let's buck the statistic here. Let's make a new statistic that *over fifty percent* of you will get serious about your business and will make the decision to bust your tails and try something new. Will you make that commitment today? Will you make a bold step today? Will you become a success story?"

Mark led the crowd by standing and clapping. He whistled, adding his noise to the cacophony erupting around him. He felt more determined than at any point in the last year. He was going to be one of those five percent. He had to be. He wouldn't wuss out. Today marked his new beginning.

"Excellent! Okay, let's get started." Todd motioned for the crowd to take their seats again. "Alright guys, I'm really excited about this first guest. Last year, he funded over three hundred units for sixty million dollars and he says he did this primarily through his social media presence along with posting videos to YouTube. Buckle up folks, you won't believe what you're going to hear."

With that brief introduction, a middle-aged man walked up to the stage, sporting a navy blue blazer, khaki slacks, and a yellow bow tie. He introduced himself as Sam Edwards and launched into a twenty minute discussion about how he'd spent about a year fully setting up his social media presence, linking it all together, and figuring out what worked and what didn't. Mark couldn't believe all the tips he was getting from Sam. Each person had been issued a Todd Duncan notepad and pen, and Mark had already filled up two pages of his signature chicken scratch. His hand ached by the time Sam stopped the presentation and asked the crowd if they had any questions. Hands shot up everywhere. Sam then spent another ten minutes answering as many questions as possible, ranging from whether they should hire someone to handle social media or if they needed to focus on one specific platform. Mark thought Sam did a great job and made a note to get his contact information before leaving the conference.

The rest of the day progressed in similar fashion. Two more speakers presented before Todd dismissed everyone to take a break and walk through the vendor hall. Mark strolled through the vendor booths, not recognizing most of the companies. There were closing gift companies, CRMs, and presentation tools to increase realtor business. Mark grabbed a few flyers from the CRM booths. He'd often heard about how important these systems were, but after the third presentation he was convinced he needed to act immediately. While wandering through the hall, he felt his pocket vibrate. Mark pulled out his phone and read: Call Me ASAP – Johnsons.

Oh, great. What does Linda need now?

This is what he'd been worried about—a work-related issue that would physically or mentally take him away from the conference. Mark stepped out of the hall into the relative quiet and tapped the processor's number.

"Hey, Mark, how's the conference?"

"It was going fine until I got the e-mail. What's going on?"

Watch your tone, Mark! This is probably your fault anyway.

Linda cleared her throat. "Well, I could tell that you spent more time on this file to get it as complete as possible. Do you remember reviewing the AUS findings?"

Mark closed his eyes and wracked his brain. He couldn't remember. He tried his best to run this on all of his files, but he couldn't specifically remember on this. "No, Linda, I don't. What did I miss?"

"Funny thing, it wasn't run at all."

"What?!" The question burst out of Mark before he could stop it.

"That's right. And now I'm getting an Approve/Ineligible because of the credit score and some late pays that are on the credit report from a year or two ago. I've tried a few different things, Mark, but it's just being stubborn. I'm not sure how to get this one through."

"Wow. I can't believe I did that." Mark was lost for words. The borrower's credit scores weren't really that low, but he'd seen this happen occasionally. They must have been late on some student loans or possibly car debt. All he remembered was that they didn't have a particularly strong report because they'd hit a rough patch and had to just make due for a while.

"The good news is you submitted this early so we've got some time to work on it, but we need to reach out to the borrower quickly to figure out how to proceed. I can't, and I mean I absolutely can't, submit this in to an underwriter without an Approve/Eligible. They're watching your files very closely."

"So, you've heard?"

A slight pause. "Yes, and I'm sorry to hear that you're having to go through this. I hope the conference helps and that you're able to sort everything out with them. In the meantime, I'll do everything I can, but please continue working hard to submit the best files possible."

"I will. I appreciate it, Linda." Mark said goodbye and hung up. Expletives ran through his mind. He wanted to shout at the top of his lungs.

Dammit! Can I just go one *file without shooting myself in the foot?*

Mark considered whether he should skip the next session and handle this issue or commit to the conference and deal with it later. He headed back to the ballroom, reasoning that it would probably be best for the client if he could have some time to think through their options. He wasn't going to cheat himself, Jennifer, or their kids because of another fire drill either.

The rest of the sessions were knockouts as well. If Todd was looking to deliver massive value, he totally succeeded by Mark's judgment. Any one of these ideas, systems, or methods could completely change Mark's business. But he realized there was a catch. These people had developed a system that worked for *them*. It either played to their strengths or they figured out what delivered the results they were looking for. Mark would need to carefully vet if he had the same talents, strengths, or desires to fully implement one or more of these strategies. It wouldn't be easy. If it was, everyone would be as successful as these guys. As the last speaker exited to massive applause, Todd got back on stage with the same level of intensity.

"Wow! Do you think this will make a difference for you? Do you think that you can go out and change your future with these tools and systems?"

The crowd went nuts and Mark threw in more of his famed whistles. The ballroom was euphoric. *Hallelujah, Lord . . . we've been delivered!*

"Okay, great! That's what I wanted to see. Right now, I'm going to talk to you about a strategy that I usually outline in more detail in Sales Academy, but I wanted to give you an overview now and whet your appetite for some of the things we discuss. It's what I call the Todd Duncan High Trust Interview. I guarantee that if you can master this technique and truly internalize the script and make it part of your daily routine, you'll be on stage with these guys next year. How does that sound?"

More thundering applause. For the next thirty minutes Todd went over the High Trust Interview. Mark was floored at how basic the concept was but how big of an impact it would have on any realtor meeting he booked moving forward.

The High Trust Interview was all about diving deep with that individual, truly understanding what they wanted from their career and in life, seeking to know what drives them and how to empower them further. The key, as Todd stressed over and over again, was to make sure you were meeting with top producers. This was a relatively lengthy process, and as a loan officer, you wanted to make sure it counted. Mark felt this was absolutely key to his future.

Some time ago, he had quit going after the top realtors because he'd limited his thinking. He didn't feel he could really deliver value outside of closing on time and was fearful he would damage relationships, precluding him from ever doing business with that realtor or broker again.

I've been living in a fear and scarcity mentality for so long that I've forgotten what it means—and how it feels—to have a strategic plan. I'm so ready to start over.

———

At thirty thousand feet, Mark replayed the last few days in his mind as he aimlessly watched the ground far below him. What an impactful weekend! He felt inspired. Charged. Capable of changing his circumstances.

His Sales Mastery workbooks and Todd's book *High Trust Selling* sat on the foldout table in front of him. This new information was a roadmap to approaching a sales career and how to make sure you didn't sacrifice what was important for what was easy. He'd already made it a quarter of the way through the book.

Mark knew there were going to be some hard days ahead. He not only needed to figure out what strategy he was going to develop to drive loans into his pipeline, but he needed to fix the ongoing issues that had been plaguing him as well. He knew a meeting with Tyler was in the works and hoped this would be the missing piece to fix his origination problems.

A few days ago, Mark had called the Johnsons after the last session. They were understandably upset, but Mark created a strategy with them that would allow them to still move forward on their house, but it would require a higher down payment. It was mostly damage control and Mark was still kicking himself for not running the AUS earlier in the process. As he sat there, lost in thought, the light bulb went off:

I need a checklist. Yes! How simple.

He remembered using a checklist when he first got into the mortgage business and was learning the ropes. Back then, he'd rarely had the issues he was facing now so it was probably time to dust off the checklist and start using that religiously—even if it meant extra time to submit a loan.

Pleased with himself, Mark turned away from the window and shifted his weight. He picked up *High Trust Selling* and turned to the page he'd earmarked.

CHAPTER 18
THE WHY OF THE WORK
45 DAYS

All was dark and quiet in Mark's house save for the light glow of his cell phone: 4:57 a.m. He was actually awake a few minutes before the alarm and was using these minutes to check Facebook and his other social media accounts. He'd posted pictures of the Sales Mastery conference over the few days he'd been in California and was pleasantly surprised to see that he had received a lot more "likes" than he had anticipated. A few were actually from real estate partners, which was great since he intended to use the posts as conversation starters in order to meet with them.

Even though it was Monday, Mark felt alert and determined to implement what he'd learned. He intended to use a portion of his Miracle Morning time to get clear on what his unique value proposition was (as Todd Duncan had called it) and figure out a strategy that worked for him. Mark recalled other methods he had tried in the past that had fallen flat because his energy quickly fizzled out when he didn't get the desired results within a few weeks.

The clock on his phone changed to 5:00 and Mark got out of bed as slowly and quietly as possible. If these changes brought success, Mark intended to buy a better bed that would allow him to sneak out without waking Jennifer so easily. Their reunion last night had been great. After putting Jason to bed, they stayed up late, catching up on what Mark had learned in California.

On the first night, Todd had stressed the importance of getting people in your life on board with your direction and goals. Mark couldn't think of a better cheerleader than Jennifer. Even now, she was attentively listening to his stories about the speakers, his goals, and what he wanted for their life. Sharing these things felt awkward at first because they felt like a fantasy to Mark, but after a few minutes both of them were actually envisioning a more abundant life together. The exercise turned out to be surprisingly fun. Jennifer even hopped off the couch, jogged to the kitchen, and came back with a legal pad and pen to take notes.

Now that's unexpected, but man does that make me want to make this all work.

Mark padded into the kitchen and grabbed a hot cup of coffee. Drink in hand, he turned toward the kitchen table and stopped mid-sip. Jennifer had organized his journal, a little Bluetooth speaker, a pen, and the book he'd been reading. The scene warmed his heart and he smiled. He couldn't get over how supportive she'd been—almost like she'd been waiting for this version of Mark to appear for years and was now doing whatever she could to encourage his growth and progress. Mark made a mental note to grab flowers for her on the way home and took a seat in front of the materials she'd laid out.

The next time Mark looked up, the sun was shining in the windows across the room and the clock read 6:15. *Wow! Time's up already?*

The past hour had been filled with a lot of writing, but not necessarily a lot of direction. Mark found it cathartic to get his thoughts out on paper, but was still frustrated to not have arrived at a clear direction. Todd's words echoed in his mind: this process could take a while, so be patient with it. Mark intended to do just that.

In his journal, he had outlined a few of the strategies both Todd and his guests had presented. Mark placed a pro and con list next to each strategy. He intended to go all-in on only one strategy but possibly carry out a secondary one, garnering the most bang for his buck without as much of a time investment. He already knew which main strategy he was leaning toward but wanted to get Tyler's input before he settled on one.

Mark decided to take a run through the neighborhood for his exercise portion of the SAVERS. If this strategy had worked for Hal when he was in his funk, surely it could work for him as well. Mark didn't particularly enjoy running, but it was the cheapest and easiest form of exercise. After changing out of his pajamas and lacing up his running shoes, Mark crept out of the house and quietly shut the front door without alerting Boomer. *God help us both if he barks!*

The early morning air was warm and muggy. *Another beautiful Texas morning.* He knew it was mostly just an excuse, but Mark felt that running outside in Texas was like running through a sauna. You never really felt like you were breathing. The air was so thick with humidity that you could almost feel the air form water deposits as you moved through it.

Mark did a little light stretching and hit the streets. In the past, he would have listened to a custom hard-rock playlist to motivate him. This morning he would try something new. He'd read once that if you play a motivational speech or something that loosely engages the mind during a run, it helps divert attention from aching muscles and lungs on fire.

During the Todd Duncan conference, he'd heard some people talking about an app called SoundCloud. Mark had downloaded it that day and found a motivational playlist. He'd only listened to one track so far, but it had definitely put him in the right mindset. Starting out was tough, but after a block or two at a moderate pace, he got into a nice rhythm. Mark switched between listening to the clips and letting his mind reflect on the changes he'd made so far.

Though he hadn't been doing the Miracle Morning routine very long, he found it to be addicting. At the very least, it made him feel like he was already accomplishing something for the day and making him a better, more focused LO. In fact, even though he hadn't had nearly as many bad days as before, the few that hit him were less severe. For the first time in a long time, he felt like he was more in control of both the situation and his emotions.

Mark made the circuit around his neighborhood in about forty-five minutes. The run had taken slightly longer than he'd thought it would, but he felt great—outside of wanting to throw up. He headed into the still-dark house and tiptoed upstairs. Waking up so early had put him ahead of schedule, so it was a great opportunity to get ready early and spend more time with the family.

As Mark stood in the shower, his soon-to-be-aching muscles welcomed the infinite stream of steaming water. *I have to get back in shape. These few extra pounds aren't my friends.* He then formulated a mental to-do list for the day ahead. One of the things he struggled with the most was call reluctance. He wasn't making enough calls therefore, he wasn't generating as much business. He pledged to call three prospective realtors and five prospective borrowers, either from his database or a new lead source. He then thought of the leads the company had purchased several years ago and decided to mine that database for anyone who might still be interested or who might have had a change of circumstances. He vowed to prospect in the morning while both he and the prospects were fresh. *Isn't that what Todd said? Deal first with the things you least want to do?* By then, he'd be ready to meet Tyler for their scheduled lunch meeting. He then promised himself he'd use the afternoon to get a status on his current pipeline and do preventative damage control before either Linda or Teri got ahold of another train wreck file.

With his shower over and a game plan for the day, Mark got out, dried off, and dressed for the day. He felt remarkably upbeat and hopeful. *Today feels like a tie day.*

There was just something about wearing a tie that made him feel more committed and professional. He'd actually noticed a spike in his productivity while wearing a tie, thus reinforcing positive behaviors.

Mark heard Jennifer clanging pans downstairs. *She must be making some eggs or bacon. I picked a good day to stick around.*

He didn't hear Jason downstairs so he headed toward his room. Stepping inside, Jason had his back turned to him and was rummaging through his dresser for clothes, humming a little tune to himself. As Mark watched him from the doorway, he marveled at Jason's inability to do anything without humming, singing, talking, or making *some* kind of sound. It was cute, but Mark was a little worried it would cause him to be disruptive in school. *I'll have to keep an ear out for that.*

"Hey, buddy, you ready for breakfast?"

Startled, Jason jumped at his dad's voice. He turned around, clothes in his hand, and said, "You bethca! Got to get dressed first."

Mark grinned and went downstairs. Jennifer was also humming something as she prepared breakfast. She smiled as he approached and wrapped him in a hug with a brief kiss. Mark liked to start his mornings like this. It made him feel complete and provided the confidence he needed for the day ahead. She was in fact making bacon, eggs, and toast, and Mark jumped in to help her prepare so he could eat with them and head out. A few minutes later, Jason joined them and sat at the kitchen table, humming to himself and playing with the salt and pepper shakers on the table.

"Daddy, will you come to my game today?"

Crap. When is it? Did I space it? Again?

He glanced at the small family calendar on the fridge. Sure enough, it was there. "Of course bud. I wouldn't miss it for the world."

Mark pretended like he didn't see Jennifer's sidelong glance.

Jason squinted at him and asked, "The whole game? Not just the last part?"

Mark pretended like his son's question didn't feel like a red-hot poker to his heart.

"Yes, I will be sure to be there for the *entire* game."

Why the hell did they have these games during the week? It wasn't enough for an adult to juggle all the things they had to do just to provide the basics, but then you throw a kid's game into the mix when it could be on the weekend? These schedules are a sure recipe for chaos, no matter what kind of parent you are.

Jennifer came up behind Mark and whispered, "I'll remind you." Mark reached out and gave her shoulder an appreciative squeeze. Fifteen minutes later, the family was laughing through forkfuls of egg and bites of bacon, talking about the last trip they'd taken.

Mark carried their dishes to the sink and gathered his things. On his way out, he bear-hugged Jason and tousled his hair. Jennifer followed him to the door.

"You're going to have a great day today, babe. Give 'em hell."

Mark smiled and pulled Jennifer close. He needed this support more than he could communicate.

CHAPTER 19
COLD CALLS AND
COLDER SHOULDERS
45 DAYS

The drive to work was uneventful. Big-city traffic was always unpredictable but luckily the only delay was just normal early morning congestion. People straggled into work as he completed his morning office ritual: making coffee and small talk. Finally, at 8:30 he sat in front of his desk, a short list of prospects on the notepad next to him. Mark took a few deep breaths and recited his affirmations: *You can do this. You are a good loan officer. These prospects will have a good experience and relationship with you. They want this relationship. They just don't know they want it yet.*

After a few rounds, Mark picked up the receiver and punched in the number for an old borrower prospect from the lead pile. The phone rang a few times and ultimately went to voicemail. Mark left a short message.

"Hi, Anthony. This is Mark Stiles with ABC Mortgage. I'm calling to see if you are looking to save money each month on your mortgage payment or perhaps looking to get pre-qualified to buy a home in today's hot market. We contacted you some time ago, but I just wanted to follow up and make sure you've been taken care of."

Mark left his contact information and hung up. It could have been better, but it certainly could have been worse. The first call was generally the hardest in his opinion. After getting a few "not interested at this time" responses and one disconnected number, he methodically worked through the remaining prospects and left messages for all of them. It was tough to know whether they were simply screening his calls or whether he'd caught them at an inconvenient time. Since it was early in the workday, they may have been playing catchup or still getting ready for work. He would try again tomorrow afternoon before leaving the office, or he might even stay late. Mark was ready to try just about anything right now to prove he was doing what it took to succeed.

He shifted his focus to the short list of realtors he wanted to contact, purposefully calling those with whom he didn't care if the conversation went well or not. According to Sales Mastery, about twenty percent or less of the agents who were actively working did eighty percent of the business. Going forward, Mark would have to be very intentional about who he contacted and how much time he spent with those individuals. In order to be as successful as possible, he would need to maximize his time with the agents who would provide him with the greatest results.

Maybe I should make a list of the agents who've given me a majority of my leads. Then I could double-down with them in addition to prospecting for top agents.

That gave Mark another idea. He pulled up his Facebook account and posted a quick sentence or two. Mark hoped it wouldn't offend anyone, but he thought this post could be a fast and unique way to gain access to realtors.

He reviewed the sentences a few times.

Hey everyone! If you've recently bought or sold a home or if you have a friend or family member who has recently sold a home, will you please let me know if the closing was delayed because of the lender? I'm looking to connect directly with those people who couldn't close because of lender issues. Private message or my e-mail is fine. Thanks!

After a few reviews, it looked good enough to post. *Maybe I'll even run a Facebook ad campaign.* Mark wrote that down in his notepad to speak with Tyler about at lunch. Turning his attention back to his list, Mark recited his brief cold-call script a few more times.

Julie, a realtor with Keller Williams, was first on his list and located a few miles away from his office. Mark knew the majority of the Keller Williams' offices in the Dallas area had a Marketing Services Agreement, which would make breaking into them difficult—not that the MSA was likely producing all that well. But, realtors routinely used an MSA as an excuse not to be bothered with loan officers looking to meet. *Comes with the territory, I guess.* Mark was going to make this as realistic as possible. He picked up the phone and fake-dialed the number. He imagined the phone ringing a few times and Julie picking up.

"Hello, this is Julie with Keller Williams."

"Hi, Julie. This is Mark Stiles with ABC Mortgage. How are you doing today?"

"Oh, hello Mark. I'm doing okay."

"Great, good to hear. Hey Julie, I know that this is a bit out of the blue, but I wanted to check on the status of your current lending relationship. Is it providing you everything that you need to be as successful as possible?"

"You know Mark, I'll be honest with you. I'm pretty happy with my

current lender. *You may not know this, but we also have an MSA in-house, and anything my existing relationship can't do, the MSA lender generally can."*

"Oh, okay. Well if anything changes, I'm happy to be a backup. I know that lender relationships can change and you may need someone to step in to save a deal. Would it be okay if I send you my contact information so you'll have it if you need it?"

"Sure, Mark. That would be fine."

"Great! If you can give me your e-mail address, I'll send it right over and I promise that it won't end up on a distribution list."

Mark imagined Julie rattling off the address, saying goodbye, and moving on. It wasn't as strong as he'd like, but if he could play the numbers game, he'd land someone who'd recently had a terrible experience.

Feeling relatively satisfied, Mark took a deep breath, dialed Julie's number. Sure enough, after two rings, Julie picked up the phone.

"Hello?"

"Hi, is this Julie with Keller Williams?"

"Yes . . . it is. Who is this?"

"This is Mark Stiles with ABC Mortgage. How are you doing today?"

"Hi, Mark. I'm doing okay. Are we working on a deal together?" Her tone was borderline snide. Whether intentional or not, she sounded irritated that Mark was calling. He did his best to move past that, but it intimidated him.

"No, we're not Julie. I was calling to see if you were satisfied with your current lending relationship?"

"Yes, I am. I need to go now if that's okay?" Very short, very to the point. She didn't want to be a part of this conversation. Honestly, Mark didn't either. *What a train wreck.*

"Sure, thank you for your time, Julie." Mark's confidence balloon deflated. He sure as hell didn't want to go through that torture again this morning. *That didn't just go poorly, it completely failed.* He would run this conversation by Tyler and hope for some direction as to what had happened.

Mark decided to move his pipeline review from later that afternoon to now. He didn't like that he was already sacrificing his schedule, but he didn't want to completely burn through the prospects he wanted to call without getting some direction. He tried to remember the last time that he'd had true sales training.

It must have been, what, five years ago? After the financial crises, the company put all the originators through the program to kick-start our originations.

Mark remembered that it had helped somewhat, but the training seemed elementary now. He needed something big and innovative that would garner direct leads and direct closings.

I don't have time to be on the wrong path.

Mark finished his last call with his borrowers, right as his alarm went off to leave and meet with Tyler. *Thank God I took the time to go through my pipeline this morning.* He'd caught some very basic errors and resolved the issues before they became problems. He made a note to ask those same questions each time he took an application to try to catch them in advance. He grabbed a notepad, his Todd Duncan materials, his *Miracle Morning* book, and stepped out of his office. Mark met eyes with a few of his colleagues.

They know I'm a dead man walking. No, I won't allow that to happen. If I leave, it'll be on my terms—not because I'm asked to. It won't come to that anyway. Right? I'm on the right path. I just need to get some course-correction in a few specific areas.

CHAPTER 20
THE BEST APP
IS A COMPLETE APP
45 DAYS

Mark and Tyler met at an unassuming local diner between their offices. The two greeted, grabbed their food, and sat down. Between bites, Tyler asked Mark about the conference and how the Miracle Morning had been going for him.

"The conference was amazing," Mark gushed. "I appreciate you being so adamant about me going because I got a lot out of it. If nothing else, it's just good to see people performing at that level and knowing it can be done. The ideas that the top performers shared were also top-notch."

"That's great to hear! I remember I was starry-eyed after my first conference, too. I felt like Saul on the road to Damascus—really eye-opening. A conversion experience of sorts. I showed up as a fairly average originator and walked away capable of conquering the industry. It completely changed the way I view and conduct my business.

I learned that there was a better way to build my business other than just sheer power of will. Did you have any specific breakthroughs?"

"You know, I actually did. Part of it happened this morning too. I realized that I need to stop hunting and start farming. When you and I first started, I took the education approach to attract referral partners and build a borrower base. At some point, I got away from that, and it just hasn't been the same since. I've decided that I'm going to take on fewer clients and referral partners but be highly intentional in those relations and begin farming with those folks."

"Wow, that's an interesting approach. We'll have to talk more about that, but that's exactly the kind of thing I hoped you would uncover."

They then moved on to discussing their Miracle Morning routines. Tyler had recently started an in-depth meditation regimen, even hiring a private trainer to help him explore meditation further. The meeting had no pre-defined time limit so Mark intended to get every ounce of help he could. He started to ask another question but Tyler cut him off.

"How would you say things have been going since we've begun meeting?"

"You know, they've actually improved a little bit, but I've only got," Mark ticked off the days in his head, "forty-five days until I'm either fired or off the hook. I've been much more conscientious about my files, but I've still made some mistakes that I shouldn't. Being aware that I have a problem has helped. Now I'm trying to figure out how to go back to the basics and start fresh. To reset."

"Good, so let's start there. It sounds to me like something is happening fairly early on in the process that's creating a ticking time bomb, ready to explode and destroy a timely closing. Talk to me about what you do when you take an application."

Mark walked Tyler through his application interview in a few minutes. Tyler listened intently and nodded slightly. Mark noticed a slight smirk.

"Okay, what am I doing wrong?"

"Not necessarily wrong, but I have a suspicion. How many years of employment and residence history do you ask for at the time of the interview?"

Mark thought. "Two years. I always ask for two years."

"Every time? What if the prospect pushes back on you that they don't remember the exact dates or location? Maybe they say they don't have a lot of time or you sense irritation so you back off."

"Hmm," Mark thought aloud. "Yeah, I guess there are times I don't push the issue very hard. I'm usually in such a hurry to get the application filled out so that I can start the process that I don't make sure that I've got the full two years for both residence and employment." *I gotta start deep diving with my borrowers.*

"And why do you think that's important?"

Mark knew Tyler was employing the Socratic method of learning and questioning, where the teacher asks the student probing questions to get them to think versus simply answering with yes or no.

"Well, obviously the employment history is important because we need to show stable earnings and that the borrower has been in the same field of work for a sufficient amount of time. I honestly don't know why it's all that important to get the residential history right, though. I just learned that I had to have it starting out and I do my best to get it."

"Okay, this is good. And believe me, Mark, I'm learning all the time myself. As originators, we need to get the two-year residential history up front first for two primary reasons. First, we may need to do a Verification of Rental or Mortgage depending on the loan requirements, especially if it's a manual underwrite. But the second and more important reason is that we're looking for whether this borrower owns property. If you ask someone whether they owned or rented a property that they vacated less than two years ago, you could have a property to include on page three of the 1003. That may open up the door to calculating rental income or loss, which may or may not be present on the tax return. Not all borrowers actually fill out their tax returns correctly, or, even scarier, have a tax preparer who does it correctly either."

Interesting. This makes a lot of sense.

Mark cringed as he recounted details of a recent deal that had blown up for similar reasons. In hindsight, he had tried blaming the borrowers for not fully disclosing that they owned other properties but now he realized, the blame was his. He hadn't asked the right questions upfront. It wasn't fair to expect borrowers to know lending guidelines. They don't know that if properties are paid off and no lien appears on a credit report, the taxes and insurance on these properties must still be counted in their qualifying debt ratios. *I will add this to my checklist of application questions.*

Tyler continued. "You still need to ask them if they own any property, including raw land. This will catch some that fall through the cracks, especially if it's happened fairly recently."

"Hmm, that definitely would help. It doesn't become a problem all the time, but one time is one time too many." Mark shifted in his seat. "While we're on the two-year history, what about employers? What do you do to make sure you've got that completely locked down?"

Tyler smiled. "This took a little bit of crafting over the years and I've got the scar tissue to prove it from deals that weren't put together right up front. When talking with a borrower, I put the most emphasis on their employment and income history. Why wouldn't you? After all, it's essentially the basis for loan qualification."

Tyler paused to let that sink in. Mark nodded his head in agreement and Tyler continued.

"I make sure to get *all* of the employer's contact information. I don't rely on the borrower to be able to produce that, especially if they've moved recently or if they have a turbulent job history. That's a red flag in and of itself, but I know the goal is mostly to show two years of solid, dependable work history."

"So what do you do if the borrower says they don't remember or it will take them a little while to track it down?"

"I don't accept it," Tyler replied flatly. "The thing is, the borrower generally doesn't understand the full gravity of the situation that you and I are in. We are constantly working against the clock, trying to overcome obstacles that aren't immediately evident at the point of application when everything appears to be rosy. So, to avoid a train wreck, I make sure we do not move past this part of the application until I have it exactly right. I pull up Google and search for the current and past employers' addresses. And I'll tell you what, Mark, I go one step further."

Tyler paused, luring Mark into asking what the extra step was. Mark obliged and Tyler answered, "I make them give me their HR contact's number."

"What? How do you do that? Why do you do that?"

"Let me ask you this, Mark. How many times have you heard from your processor that they can't get a hold of the company HR person or that they keep getting the runaround?"

"Too many times."

"Exactly. Why make them work extra hard on something that I can get right now? This is the one area I'll let go unanswered on the phone with the prospect because they may literally not have access to this. But I'll tell you what. If they're at work, in front of a computer, I ask them to reach out to everyone who might be able to track that information down so that by the time we're done with the application, I've got a good contact number. If need be, I'll call in advance of submitting the application to make sure I've tracked the right person down."

"So, let me get this straight. During or shortly after the application, you gather *every* bit of information about the employer, including the HR contact?"

"Yep, that's exactly right. Street address, suite number, phone number, the whole shebang."

"Isn't that the processor's job?" Mark wasn't trying to be difficult, but if his task was to bring in business, wasn't it the processor's job to handle the nitty-gritty details?

"Mark, do you really want to put both your reputation and your income in the hands of another person? It doesn't matter how competent or capable they are. Do you want to give up that control?"

Mark hadn't thought about this before. He clearly saw the value now. There were things he could be and should be doing up front that would not only save time but would also ensure the loan closed on time as well. Even if it took him a few extra minutes or even an hour, the nightmare it would prevent later in the process would be well worth the time expense.

"Okay, I'll start doing that from now on." Mark scribbled a few notes.

Tyler waited until he had Mark's full attention.

CHAPTER 21
WHEN INCOME LEADS TO BAD OUTCOMES
45 DAYS

"Now, let's get to the meat of the application. I told you just a minute ago that I spend the most time during the initial discussion with the prospect figuring out their income. Walk me through what you do."

Mark jumped right in. "Well, I think I've got this pretty much locked down." He paused when he saw Tyler smirk again. "I do, I swear!" Mark insisted. Tyler motioned for him to continue.

"I start the conversation by finding out what the borrower does. That tells me whether they are salaried or self-employed. When we get to the income section of the application, I then ask how often they get paid and what their income is. I back into the number a few ways to make sure that the annual figure they're telling me matches up to their earnings on each pay check."

Tyler nodded, but it was clear more questions were coming. "So, you ask them how often and how much they get paid to determine their salary? Do you ever ask to see a paycheck prior to the application or call?"

"No, I usually don't ask for anything until I'm absolutely certain I've got a viable loan application."

"So, you're judging whether you have a viable loan based on what someone verbally tells you who may or may not have *ever* done this process before?"

Mark winced at that logic. "Hmm. I suppose it would make more sense to ask for that income documentation up front and then I can confirm what I see with them."

"That's exactly what you need to start doing from this moment on. Again, this was a lot of trial and error over the years, but I kept hitting a wall when it came to income, especially when the debt-to-income ratio was right on the edge of qualifying. They'd tell me they were strictly salary, but sure enough, when the pay stubs and Verification of Employment would come rolling in, I'd have bonus or commission income in there, and it would either complicate or blow up the deal. And to our borrowers' credit, I've never had someone try to be dishonest with me. They just don't understand that the make-up of their income is absolutely crucial."

"Okay." Mark bit his bottom lip as he took more notes and muttered, "Always base income on what they provide, *not* what they tell you. How do *you* go about doing this?"

"Great question. I actually ask for the borrower to provide me with all of this information *prior* to taking the application. In fact, I essentially complete the 1003 prior to speaking with them in ninety-five percent of my business. That way, we're simply reviewing and fact-checking every single line of the application to make sure I've got the most accurate information possible."

"Wait, wait, wait. You ask your borrowers for *all* of their information before even taking the application? And you actually *get* it?"

"Yep." Tyler's smirk widened into a broad smile.

"The tax returns, bank statements, ID's, pay stubs, *everything?*"

Tyler nodded his head to each item. Mark was in disbelief.

Surely Tyler isn't telling the whole truth. I've never met a loan officer who actually gathers that stuff in advance, let alone asks for it. But the logic's so sound! How easy would it be to just verify all of the information once you've received it prior to giving any sort of assurance that someone was pre-qualified?

"So how do you do this? How do you ask for the documents?"

"Honestly Mark, at this point, I don't so much ask as I command politely. I've worked with my referral partners long enough that when I tell them I must have all of these documents in advance of taking an application, they work with the customer to gather that stuff in advance too. They know that if I can get all of this information up front, I can deliver on my part. Additionally, when I'm handed a referral, I immediately have the contact's information uploaded to my Customer Relationship Management tool so I've got the e-mail queued up to go out. I'll set you up in my CRM so that you can see what it looks like."

"Wow, that would be great. I'm going to try to do this as often as I can. But, what if you absolutely can't convince the prospect to visit you face-to-face?"

"It does happen from time to time, but I do everything I can to convince them otherwise. I've had folks travel thirty minutes one way just to meet. It's never a matter of whether or not they can. It's whether they feel like it's worth it or not. If you can teach your referral partners why it's so important to meet face-to-face, they'll help make sure it happens. If the client absolutely refuses, I'll do the transaction electronically." Tyler paused for a moment and then added wryly, "Another bonus to this method is that you'll be spending so much time with your prospect that they can't *imagine* repeating the process with another lender. Even over the phone." With that, he took a sip of tea and winked.

Mark took a few more notes while Tyler continued. "Now, let's keep going on the income. We're still not done with the salaried prospect yet."

Mark furrowed his brow.

Not done with the salaried prospect yet? Their pay stubs are all you really need to worry about.

"I'm not following you. What's left?"

"Surely you've had salaried borrowers who supplied you with a wonderful Schedule C that had *substantial* losses from a little side venture? Or, how about 2106 expenses?"

Oh, yeah, the fly in the ointment. Tax return schedules were like blood clots just waiting to dislodge and cause an aneurism in the life of a loan. I've had so many borrowers forget, or just not understand, how their tax returns were filled out. They didn't realize that it mattered. But it mattered. A lot.

"Geez, yeah I forgot about that. I'm dealing with a loan like that right now. The borrower has a little side business that popped up in the latest tax return. Working to get that issue resolved."

"See! You had a viable loan *until* you figured out that there were losses to deal with. Imagine knowing that up front and coaching your prospects through the implications of those tax returns on their qualifying income. Again, all documents up front is a game changer."

Man, this was great stuff. Why the hell wasn't anyone teaching this? Maybe they were and he just missed the memo?

"Okay, anything else for us to cover with salaried borrowers?"

"No, I think that's pretty much it. You're going to have your nuances to deal with, but I'd say the majority of issues fall into what we've talked about."

After taking a drink, Mark kept the conversation moving, wanting to absorb everything he possibly could. "All right, so let's talk about self-employed and rental properties. I've learned a few things here, but I'm sure you can shine light on the areas I'm missing."

"It may seem weird, but let's role play this. I'll be, say, Kevin, and I'm a self-employed borrower. We're talking about income now."

Mark grinned awkwardly. It was a bit strange, but Tyler clearly had his act together, so he was willing to be uncomfortable.

"Hey Kevin, I need to know how much you reported last year on your tax returns?"

"Well, I made a hundred-thousand dollars," Tyler/Kevin responded.

"Wow, that's great. Good year?"

"Yeah, it was better than last year. Pretty much doubled my sales."

"Good, glad to hear things are going well." Mark paused, waiting for Tyler to say something.

Tyler stepped out of character. "That's it? No additional probing?"

"I asked him what he made and determined that there was actually increasing income. I should be able to average the two years if it's increasing.

Tyler shook his head. "You're right about the averaging of income if it's increasing, but you asked me what I reported on my tax returns. That could mean anything. To the borrower trying to qualify for a home, they're trying to paint themselves in the best light possible. At no point did you figure out if it was gross or net income that Kevin was talking about. Additionally, you assumed that his net income increased because he said he doubled his sales. There could have been more than twice as much expense associated with generating that income. Again, this is why it's so crucial to have these tax returns. In addition to the net income, you need to know what expenses can be added or subtracted."

Mark scribbled again. *Yep, I've had a deal or two blow up for this reason.*

"You just said expenses had to be subtracted. How's that possible if we're already dealing with net income?"

"Because of the meals and entertainment deduction on the Schedule C. That deduction he's showing is what the IRS will allow him to take. You need to actually double that and reduce qualifying income because the borrower's true cash flow was lower. Now, on the other hand, if he has car expenses, you need to dig into those because you may be able to add back additional depreciation expense on conventional loans. You *must* know the guidelines of the loan program with self-employed borrowers because you don't get that luxury with VA or FHA loans. Again, the first rule of being a good LO is: **LEARN. THE. GUIDELINES.**"

Perhaps I should register for one of the many ongoing self-employment training webinars instead of just depending on my underwriter to analyze tax returns.

As frustrated as Mark was that he'd committed some of these mistakes before, he was beginning to see an opportunity here.

"Tyler, do you ever meet with realtors to talk about qualifying income?"

Tyler smiled and nodded his head. "Of course I do! This shows them I'm the expert and that they need to send their clients to *me* and only *me* in order to get their commissions on time and make their clients happy."

Mark made a note to look into that.

"And I'll give you another tip," Tyler continued. "Go ahead and get licensed with the Texas Real Estate Commission to offer continuing education credits. This will help legitimize and boost attendance at your gatherings. Partnering with title companies will help too."

"I feel like I should be paying you for this kind of advice."

"No need," Tyler responded. "We're friends and I enjoy helping people who are committed to changing. There's plenty of business to go around."

With legs bouncing under the table in excitement, Mark asked Tyler for his pointers on rental property income.

"You've really got to watch out for rental properties. The tax return may show income for the year, but after adding and subtracting the necessary expenses **PER THE GUIDES**, you could actually be dealing with a deal killing loss. My best advice here is to immediately reach out to your underwriter or processor to see if they have a tool for calculating rental income or loss. Most investors will have an Excel schedule that will do the heavy lifting for you. Just remember that the tax return doesn't account for principal payments on the loan and that the income will likely be limited due to a vacancy factor."

Tyler checked his watch. "We've got about ten minutes before I need to head to my next appointment. I think we've covered some good stuff here. Anything else you want to chat about?"

Mark let out a deep breath. He felt like he could sit here for hours re-educating himself on how to take a good application and jump-start his business. Just then, he remembered his realtor call from earlier that morning. *I know I have production issues, but I have to change my sales tactics too.*

"Yeah, I'd like to get your thoughts on calling realtors. I called one this morning completely out of the blue and got a really poor response. I prepared myself in advance, but it didn't go the way I wanted at all."

"You hit the nail right on the head and answered your own question. You called the realtor completely out of the blue. You didn't know her so you had no reference. She could have been doing anything before or during your call. She may have just had a fight with a spouse, a loan could have blown up, a listing could have fallen through, she might have a sick kid, whatever. She knew you were trying to sell her *on the spot.* Did you give your Unique Value Proposition that you learned at Sales Mastery?"

Mark sighed. "No, I didn't even get a chance to. I got shut down right away."

"Okay. I think this is a relatively easy fix. Todd teaches this and I swear by it for my success. You need to contact your best realtor partner and title company and ask them who they will refer you to so you can provide the same outstanding level of service you've been providing them. If you do it this way, you'll have a warm lead and can name drop the person who referred you so you can get past ever-suspicious initial gatekeepers."

Mark had taken this approach before with some mixed success, but anything would be better than what he had done this morning. *Maybe I haven't approached it right before. Maybe I've never approached it right.*

"Oh, and to ensure that your approach is successful, make sure you write a script and memorize it. Again, this is another Todd Duncan method. If you're completely prepared for that call and not merely winging it, the chances of it going south on you are greatly reduced. Role play through potential objections and come up with responses that turn those objections into something you can easily dismiss. If you're prepared, it's pretty hard for you to lose."

Tyler checked his watch again. "Alright, Mark. I've got to get going. I really enjoyed this, and think we should meet again here at the end of the week to discuss what worked and some more details about the process." Mark agreed and they parted ways.

The whole way back to the office, Mark was deep in thought.

How have I not been doing the things that we talked about today? How ludicrous! It's all so basic! I've allowed myself to stray because I can get away with it, but also because I've lost sight of the importance of the application. I've always been so focused on just hitting the closing date that I've never stepped back to think about the easiest way to accomplish that.

Mark was surprised that he actually looked forward to his next prospecting call. He planned to take the best, most thorough application of his life. He imagined Linda's reaction when she received it. *Wouldn't that give her and the other processors something to take back up the ladder?*

Mark spent the rest of the afternoon writing up notes about the conversation he'd had with Tyler and drafting scripts for his calls tomorrow. He was so into playing out the scripts that he ignored the buzzing of his phone the first few times. Finally, frustrated, he picked up the phone and stared slack-jawed at the screen.

"Oh, God," Mark moaned.

Mark grabbed his phone and keys and bolted, leaving his computer and briefcase in the office. He'd either come back to retrieve them this evening to wrap up some work or he'd be dealing with the aftermath of this latest screw up so it wouldn't matter. As he neared the exit to the parking garage, Mark pulled up the latest text from Jennifer: **If you're not here on time, all hell is going to break loose when we get home.** *Why didn't I set the alarm on my phone to remind me about the game?!*

Mark cursed and sprinted to his car. He'd be late, but only slightly so if traffic was light. He briefly considered running his car into a nearby pole so he could have an excuse, but decided against it. The headache created would be much worse than the disappointment from Jason and the thrashing he was sure to take from Jennifer.

Mark prayed for a quick trip and punched it out of the garage—right into bumper-to-bumper, horns blaring, standstill traffic.

CHAPTER 22
LATE FILES AREN'T THE WORST THAT CAN HAPPEN
44 DAYS

The aftermath of what would later be called "The Final Straw" was not pretty.

Mark had arrived at Jason's game five minutes before halftime—far too late. To Mark's pride and horror, Jason had actually scored the only goal of the game. His team was currently up 1-0 over one of the toughest teams in little league. When Mark ran up to Jason at halftime to congratulate him, Jason's chin quivered and he turned away, avoiding any eye contact with his dad. Jennifer certainly wasn't averting her gaze, though. Instead, a thoroughly irate, fuming Mama Bear glared a burning a hole through him.

Jason's team fought a hard game but lost 2-1 on a last-minute goal by a kid who looked several grades ahead of the rest. The loss had broken their hearts and there were few dry eyes on the field as the little boys sought the comfort of their parents. Every other parent regaled Mark during the entire game about how Jason had scored the goal.

Thankfully, one parent had recorded the game, but it would be forever branded as the one game Mark missed that had really counted.

The ride home was no better. Mark tried to lighten the mood a few times but never received a response. The silence was deafening. *Maybe I should've let Jennifer and Jason ride back with the couple they had carpooled with.*

He hoped the quiet ride home would give them a chance to cool off, but he was wrong. As soon as they got home, Jennifer heated up leftovers and drew a bath for Jason—all without a single glance or word to Mark. Still in his work clothes, Mark plopped down in the living room, not sure what to do next. *They're both tired of listening to my excuses.* Jason and Jennifer clearly weren't going to talk to him, so he was likely on his own this evening. He didn't want to turn on the TV for fear of appearing to downplay what was clearly a precarious situation. The same was true if he tried to crack open a book. To make matters worse, he didn't have his work things. *Rushing out of the office was a poor choice.*

He briefly considered leaving to go get his work, but he'd likely be gone for an hour or so, and he damned sure didn't want it to appear like he was dodging the family—again. Mark instead settled on changing into some clothes to attend to a yard in desperate need of attention. *Plus, it's scorching hot, which may give Jennifer some solace that not only am I mentally suffering, but my body's taking some heat as well. Literally.*

After an hour, Mark was satisfied with the work he'd put into the yard and ventured inside. Jennifer and Jason had already finished dinner. He heard them giggling as she put Jason down for bed. Jennifer had apparently worked her "mom magic" and gotten their son into a slightly better mood. He'd go up after Jennifer had finished their time together.

While waiting, Mark heated the remaining leftovers. Jennifer had conveniently not prepared a plate for him. His appetite wasn't great due to the heat of the situation (both family-wise and weather-wise) and despite the horrible feeling he had from missing Jason's shining moment, he forced some food down. As he mechanically moved bite after bite to his mouth and chewed, Mark reflected on why he struggled so much to keep easy, simple promises like showing up to his son's game on time. He wasn't late for lunch with Tyler today. He wasn't late to meetings at work or outside the office. He wasn't late to Dr. appointments. Hell, he was never even late to his regularly scheduled haircuts. *What the hell is wrong with me?*

It certainly wasn't for lack of love. He'd die for Jennifer and Jason. After a while, he surmised that not being able to keep his promised boiled down to priorities. Plain and simple. For some time now, Mark had been putting his work ahead of his family. He initially rationalized this need when he was first married: *I have to work hard to provide for my family.* But over time, he realized it had become a habit and he used the crutch that they would understand when he sacrificed family time because of work. Working hard (and not smart) was addicting because that was actually easier. If he would just take the time to prioritize his day and keep his commitments, he wouldn't be running into this problem again and again. Like Jennifer had so eloquently pointed out last time, it was a true integrity issue. Moving forward, he needed to make sure he was actually doing what he said he was going to do. As Stephen Covey put it, Mark wasn't making deposits into his emotional bank account with his family, which made sense since he felt emotionally bankrupt at the moment.

Mark finished and put his dishes in the dishwasher. Jennifer and Jason were still going strong so he hopped into the shower. The heat and pressure cleared his thoughts. He formulated a calendar to make along the lines of what he'd read a few days earlier in *The 7 Habits of Highly Effective People*. If he could stick to that calendar and plan his week in advance, he could make sure he was making his family commitments, setting appointments with referral partners, and not get bogged down by simply responding to e-mails and wasting time on social media. Mark mentally put the finishing touches on his soon-to-be-real calendar, shut the water off, and stepped outside to dry off. In the bedroom, he heard Jennifer opening and closing dresser drawers with much more force than normal. Probably to put laundry away. He hoped.

Mark walked over to the dresser. Jennifer brushed past him without a word or eye contact. He may as well have been invisible.

Oh, hell. I'm about to get ripped the next time I step into this room.

He slipped on some basketball shorts and a shirt and headed to Jason's room. Behind the slightly closed door, Mark heard his son softly humming a theme song from his favorite cartoon. His spirits seemed up. Mark stepped inside. Jason immediately stopped humming. A scowl came over his face and he turned his back to Mark. A pang hit Mark's stomach. He sat on the edge of Jason's bed, still facing Jason's back.

"Hey buddy, let's talk."

"I don' wanna."

"Okay, I'll start. First, I'm really, really sorry I missed part of your game today. I don't have any excuses, and I should have been there to watch you the whole time. I promise that I'll make the next one."

"No, you won't." Jason shook slightly, clearly trying to stifle his crying.

"Jason, I'm so sorry son. Why are you crying?" *Have my stupid actions completely destroyed my son?*

Finally, Jason faced him, tears streaming down his cheeks. "Because you make me feel bad! I wanted you to be there and you weren't. You promised you would be!" His little voice broke but he finished. "Daddy, I scored my first goal ever and it was even against the best team. And you missed it! I thought you cared!" Jason buried his face in his pillow and sobbed.

Mark swallowed hard as tears welled in his eyes. *Good Lord, I can't start crying also!*

But Jason's words had gut-punched him—hard. His lack of integrity was literally ruining his relationship with his precious son, one broken promise at a time. His emotional bank account with Jason was zero, possibly even negative at this point. Mark was going to have to do a lot to build that trust back up and create a positive balance.

Mark stood up, plucked Jason from the bed, and embraced him tightly. Jason was still sobbing, but he wrapped his arms around his dad's neck. Mark squeezed his son tighter and swayed with him in the darkness. He didn't know how long that lasted, but after a while Jason's breathing became regular and his arms loosened around his dad's neck. He'd fallen asleep. Mark carefully laid him down in his bed and brought the covers up over his sleeping body. Rubbing his face, Mark breathed a deep sigh and turned to leave the room.

Wow! What a mess!

The last thing he needed right now were additional problems to pile on top of his worries at work. He knew he needed to devote more time to his family, but it couldn't have come at a worst possible time for his work. Mark entered their bedroom with a sense of foreboding. He didn't have any fight in him after what had just happened. *I'm going to be a human punching bag for Jennifer's certain verbal assault.*

To his relief, the lights were off and she was in bed with her back facing his empty spot. *She's all out of fight too.* Mark got ready for bed and slipped in beside Jennifer's motionless form. Just as he was drifting off, Jennifer's pointed question brought him back to the Land of Consciousness and Disappointment.

"Where the hell were you today?"

"At the office. I just lost track of time. Plain and simple."

"How could you do that to him again? I even tried to call and text you, but as usual, I got *zero* response." The fight was building in Jennifer's voice.

Mark knew there was no sense in defending himself, and right now he didn't think he could muster the will. "I know Jen, I screwed up. I'm going to get better about getting to his games."

"It's not *just* the games, Mark." Jennifer sprang out of bed and started pacing. Mark sat up as her pot finally boiled over.

"You've done this for years to me, but now, Jason? Really? You're probably going to do it to our new baby as well! It's clear we aren't as important as your work, but how's that working out for you? You've put all this focus into *your* career and *your* success, and we just get the scraps of what you bother to give us!"

Whoa! Where did this person come from? She's been so supportive over the last few years and especially this past month. Has she been harboring these feelings the whole time, or was this brought on because of the new baby?

"What else are you talking about?"

"This didn't just start with Jason's games. This has been a running theme throughout our marriage. Late to dates, not engaging with me when we're together, always on your phone, not taking the initiative to do anything creative. I'm just sick of it! And if you can't give two people some quality time, how in the hell are you going to give *three* people quality time?!"

"Now, hold on just a minute." Mark threw back the covers and stood up.

"Don't even bother!" Jennifer hissed, trying to keep her voice low, clearly still furious. "Either you're sleeping in the guest room or I am."

"No, now stop." Mark tried to reason with her.

"Apparently I am! And guess what else? You're on my shit list until you fix things with Jason and prove to me that your family is as important—or more important—than your career!"

Jennifer slammed the door behind her. Mark heard her shut the guest bedroom door and the lock click in place. He stood in the darkness for a full minute staring blankly at the door.

What the hell just happened?

———

Mark's alarm sounded several times the next morning. Each time, Mark silenced the ringing, rolled over, and went back to sleep. He'd spent most of the night tossing and turning, re-playing the evening back over and over in his mind. Finally, around 2:00 a.m., Mark must have drifted off to sleep. That was the last time he remembered looking at his bedside clock. Now it was 7:00 and he felt awful. It was only Wednesday, but he was ready for it to be Saturday. The energy he'd been operating on had been completely drained out of him yesterday. Jennifer likely wouldn't be supporting him from here on out, and he needed to earn back Jason's trust—all the while working to keep his job.

Sluggishly, Mark went through the motions of getting ready for work. The house was silent as he left the bedroom for the garage. Passing by the guest room, the door was open, but the lights were off. Mark ducked in to see if Jennifer was there, but the room was empty, the bed made.

Hmm, very odd.

He had expected the cold shoulder today, but not waking up to an empty house. Next, he moved to Jason's room, but it too was dark and silent. Downstairs, there was little evidence anyone else even occupied the house. The kitchen was clean and put together, no telltale breakfast dishes in the sink. *Had Jennifer slipped downstairs last night to clean and clear her mind? Did she wake up early this morning? Where were they?* His morning was getting more bizarre with each passing moment. His routine was completely off. It was going to take a good deal of focus today to keep his mind off of this personal fiasco. Mark fully expected to find a farewell note on the kitchen counter or the door to the garage, but both places were clear.

Okay, I need to call her to figure out what's going on.

After the third attempt and no answer, Mark left a message for her to call him as soon as she could. He had no idea what last night's fight meant, lost as to what to do next.

Should I call her parents? Surely that's where she's gone. Would that make things worse between us? Would I get fired for not showing up to the office? Will I get fired from my marriage if I don't skip work and pursue them?

Finally, he went to the office, deciding Jennifer would let him know what the next step was in his personal life.

CHAPTER 23
IMPENDING UNEMPLOYMENT
43 DAYS

The ride to work was sobering. Mark even kept his normal motivation podcasts off in favor of driving in silence. He felt like brooding. He knew he needed to shake this funk, but he hadn't had a fight with Jennifer like this since before Jason was born.

By the time he arrived at the office and sat in front of the computer he'd meant to take home last night, he'd mostly gotten his head on straight. Here were the facts: he'd made a huge mistake by not keeping his word, what had happened was in the past, and there was nothing he could do about it now.

All I can do now is work on my integrity every single day with every action I take. Yeah, it'll be tough, but the alternatives aren't acceptable. That should help with both my family situation and work, right?

His borrowers, realtors, and other referral partners would certainly benefit from his newfound commitment to integrity. The design he came up with last night worked its way up from the depths of his mind and he sketched it in his notepad. Mark had developed a pretty good relationship with Stan, the head of their internal marketing department. The resulting sketch was straight out of Stephen Covey's *7 Habits*.

The calendar would help Mark prioritize and schedule his most important events first. By doing this, he'd be sure to accomplish the daily tasks that would bring him closer to his ultimate goals. The calendar would also allow him to dictate what his day would look like a week in advance. There was even a spot for goals. Mark lifted his head up and reviewed his work. *Not too bad.* Sticking to something like this would help keep him focused and make sure he never missed an important appointment again. *Or another soccer game.*

Determined, Mark grabbed the sketch off his desk and strode across the office to Stan's cubicle. After a brief discussion, Stan agreed to get Mark a draft of the calendar later that day. On his way back to his office, Mark considered what it would be like if every employee in the company had his calendar on their desk—a true Cinderella turnaround story, a schmuck on the brink of getting fired to a superstar employee who not only commanded a respectable sales record but also innovated and made the company better.

Before getting back to his office, David flagged Mark down from across the room. Stepping into David's office, Mark took a deep breath and tried not to sigh too loudly.

"Mark, we're two weeks into our probationary period, and I haven't seen a whole lot of change on your part. Is there something that I'm not seeing?"

What do I tell him? What's he looking for here? Just the facts, Jack, nothing more.

"Well, I think I'm off to a good start, David. I lost a little time going to the conference, and it's not like I could completely change my methods at the drop of a hat. I'm meeting regularly with my mentor and working hard to implement what I've learned. In another week or two, you should see some positive results."

"Hmm, I was hoping for something a little more substantive than that, Mark. You realize we're not joking about your performance record, right? This isn't a scare tactic. Your job is on the line."

"I fully understand where things stand, David. You reminding me of my impending unemployment is really getting me fired up."

"There's no need to be sarcastic, Mark." David paused, searching for how to proceed next. "I suppose that wasn't helpful. Is there anything you need from me?"

"No, but I do appreciate the offer." Now Mark sighed without the sarcasm. "I just need to get through the next week or two and I think things will turn around. I'll let you know if I need something."

Mark got up and walked out of David's office. He wasn't sure whether the conversation was over or not, but he didn't see it going anywhere.

Resettled at his desk, Mark scanned the new messages in his inbox. *Nothing from Jennifer.* At the top of the stack was an e-mail from Linda. Its subject line read: "Great Work – Keep It Up." Eagerly, Mark scanned the message. Words like "nice improvement" and "much cleaner file" leapt off the screen. Mark felt a warming in his chest, and the hair on his arms stood up. Not only had Linda sent the message to him, but she'd copied David and Paul.

Man, talk about perfect timing! Too bad I didn't see David until after this e-mail went out. Maybe I should print this out and go back in. Nah . . . let him see it and realize that I AM making progress.

Linda was referring to the first loan application Mark had sent her way after he'd gotten back from the Sales Mastery conference. It certainly was an improvement from what he'd done in the past.

If they're impressed by this, they haven't seen anything yet.

CHAPTER 24
THE QUALITY AND EFFICIENCY INITIATIVE
43 DAYS

Mark anticipated the next opportunity to take an application using Tyler's method. *But first things first. I need to find where in the world Jennifer went.*

Although troubled by Jen and Jason's mysterious disappearance, he felt somewhat invigorated and jotted down a few action items for the day. First, check in with Jennifer AGAIN and see if he could get some response from her about where she'd gone, when she'd be back, and what their next steps looked like. Next, list all referral partners with whom he enjoys a great relationship, reach out to them direct-ly, and solicit connections while explaining his new way of doing business. He decided to stop after these two items. Connecting with Jennifer hopefully wouldn't take long, but if he did the second item right, that could take all day. Next to that item, he listed his most important partners first and worked down the list of all the realtors and title companies he'd done loans with this year. Once the list was complete, Mark called Jennifer. After four rings, it went to voicemail.

"Hi, you've reached Jennifer Stiles' voicemail. I can't take your call right now, but if you'll leave me a message, I'll get back to you. Have a blessed day."

Mark sighed and started, "Hey Jen, it's me. I know you're upset, but not letting me know where you're at is not helping. I'm starting to get really worried because I haven't heard back from you. Please, please, call, text, or e-mail me when you get this. I love you. Tell Jason I love him as well. Bye."

Mark hit the red phone icon to hang up, stared at the blank screen, and felt suddenly empty. The good mojo from Linda's e-mail had taken a backseat to a fresh wave of guilt. After a few moments he shook his head and put the phone away. He muttered under his breath, "Okay, Mark, you gotta get it together today. Don't use this as an excuse to not do what you must do to get your life back on track." *Who am I, Todd Duncan?*

He shut his eyes and took a few deep breaths, imagining leaving the office later that afternoon satisfied with the full and productive day he'd put in. With one final deep breath, he opened his eyes and moved back to his computer. As a last ditch effort to make sure that Jen and Jason were doing alright, he checked Facebook Messenger. With any luck, there would be recent activity and he could gain some assurance that they were OK. Sure enough, Jen's profile had been active twelve minutes ago. Satisfied that he'd done all he could for now, he turned his attention to the second task.

His first call of the day was to Kelly Davis at Keller Williams. Over the last year, Kelly had consistently provided him with at least two quality leads per month. Mark had successfully closed them all so he was fairly certain this was going to be an easy call. As he picked up the phone, he paused. He didn't have a name for this new initiative. Unsure, he put the phone back on the receiver. This new method was about doing a better job and producing a higher quality file and experience for his customers. Not only would the new procedures ensure better file quality, but they would also make the process more efficient for all involved. *Quality. Efficient.* Mark put the two together and called it the Quality and Efficiency Initiative. *I like the sound of that. Q&E for short.* Pleased with himself, he punched in Kelly's number from memory. She picked up the phone almost immediately.

"Hey there, Mark. How ya doin', sir?" Kelly's signature West Texas twang sounded genuinely happy to talk to Mark.

"Hey, Kelly. I'm doing great. How's your week going?"

"Oh, just hustlin'. As usual. I'm glad you called though! I just spoke with someone that's ready to put an offer on a house and I recommended they speak with you first."

Mark lit up. "Oh, wow, thank you very much, Kelly! I really appreciate that."

"Well, you know you're my guy, hon," Kelly drawled. "What did you have on your mind this mornin' . . . or are you a mind reader?"

Mark chuckled. "Nope, definitely not a mind reader. I actually wanted to call and talk to you about a new way of doing business and how it can greatly enhance the experience that our mutual customers have. Do you have just a minute?"

"Well, sure. What do you mean a new way of doing business?"

"I'm calling it the Quality and Efficiency Initiative."

"Oh, I like that. Quality and Efficiency Initiative. That sounds fancy."

"Hah, well, thank you. I'm calling it Q & E for short. I developed it with a colleague of mine after attending a mortgage conference I attended recently. I think it's going to completely change the level of service I can provide to both my customers and my referral partners."

"That sounds great. How does it work?"

"Basically, I'm going to dive much deeper with all of my customers upfront and take the highest quality, most detailed application possible. There is a lot of crucial information that sometimes gets missed so by taking a little more time upfront to ask the right questions, I can avoid those last-minute surprises that nobody likes." Mark paused apprehensively but Kelly didn't appear too concerned.

"Makes perfect sense, go ahead, Mark. I'm listening."

"This will make the process go much smoother and get files in and out of underwriting much more quickly. In addition to this, I'm committed to collecting everything, and I mean everything, upfront from my borrowers so I can make sure there are no blow-ups."

"Oh, okay . . ." Kelly sounded confused. "But how is that different than what you do now?" Bless her cute little nasal twang.

"So glad you asked! This is where you come in, Kelly, this is where the team concept begins. In order for me to get everything I need upfront, I really need to meet with these clients face-to-face, and I need them to provide me everything at the time of that meeting. That may seem intimidating, overkill or a waste of your client's time, but I can virtually eliminate any issues with their loan and provide them the best homebuying experience possible. Imagine if your clients were raving about your service as well as the service of the people you've referred them to before they even close? Then imagine they're able to actually close early because we not only addressed any potential issues but we also provided the majority of underwriting conditions upfront? Can you imagine getting a clear-to-close with just two underwriting submissions?"

Kelly heard the passion in Mark's voice. "Hmm . . . I see where you're goin' with this. By gettin' all this stuff upfront, you don't hafta ding-dong our customer for more and more documentation every time your underwriter looks at the file . . ." Mark winced at her perception. "So it sounds like I need to prep my clients to meet with you in person instead of just gettin' them to call you?" *Wow, she doesn't sound put out at all. Does she really get it?*

"That's exactly right. Of course, if there's a reason why we absolutely can't meet, I will continue to do everything electronically. Just so you know, I will still request all documentation upfront within a limited timeframe though. The point I'm making Kelly, is if they meet me in person, they're going to have a first-class experience. The Jerry Maguire experience."

"Jerry Maguire, Huh?" Kelly laughed. "This sounds great, Mark. I'll do all I can to help with Q&E. I'll call the client that I just mentioned and ask them to schedule time to meet with you in the next day or two. Was there anything else?"

"That's it for Q & E, but I did learn a technique from Todd Duncan that I think is going to supercharge our businesses."

"Whoo! Now you're talkin' my language. What's the technique?"

"It's called the Consumer Referral Program. Basically, since I collect information from banks, CPAs, attorneys, and insurance companies, I'll be creating a network of referral partners with *you* as the *only* contact for their real estate needs. It'll be similar to a networking program, only better because I'll be conducting all the traffic, and you should get a more constant flow of referrals from the individuals I'll be working with. How does that sound?"

Mark could almost hear Kelly's eyes widen over the phone. "We'll don't that just beat all? This is some good stuff. I like this post-conference Mark!"

They bantered for a few more minutes. Mark thanked Kelly for her time and trust and hung up the phone. A smile crept across his face. *That went much smoother than expected.* He must have been holding his breath or talking too fast because his heart was racing. That one call was the perfect positive reinforcement he needed to continue making calls today. He made a note to journal about that tomorrow and add it to his affirmations. According to Hal, affirmations need to have an emotional backing or a physical attribute or else they are just empty words repeated aloud. While the memory was still fresh,

Mark played it back in his mind. As he reflected on the end of the conversation, he felt like cursing.

"Shoot! I forgot to ask for an introduction to another agent!" Mark wrote that down on the pad next to him so he could move through *every* step on his next call. He was surprised he'd forgotten to ask for a referral since that WAS one of the primary purposes of the call, after all!

The rest of the morning flew by. Mark made eight separate sales calls to real estate agents and title companies he'd worked with and received three immediate connections to follow up with. It had been a long time since he'd been this excited to make sales calls. Sure, they were fairly easy, and he wasn't asking for anything big from his referral partners, but it was a move in the right direction.

As he was finishing his notes from the last call, Mark's stomach rumbled. He didn't want to interrupt his streak, but he was also afraid to let his physical energy get down. Since he had begun monitoring his performance and energy, Mark had noticed a huge difference in his drive and willingness to do difficult tasks depending on what and when he'd eaten. He was now faced with the typical dilemma: go downstairs and grab his favorite lunch or eat two-day-old leftovers still sitting in the lounge fridge. Today, with "The Final Straw" fresh on his mind, the decision was easy. Mark didn't want to eat what he was about to eat, but he needed to as an important, small step toward continuous integrity.

While the microwave zapped his food, Mark reflected on what Stephen Covey says about integrity. In order to build up the habit of integrity, you have to continuously reinforce the actions needed to carry it out. So, by eating his lunch here and not spending money, he was making a deliberate decision to do what he said he was going to do. The same was true of the calls he was making and of the promises he made to his borrowers and referral partners. If he could just honor the little things, it would build him up to honor his more difficult decisions.

A short time after finishing lunch, Mark got his first opportunity to exercise his new Q&E technique. True to form, Kelly's referral had reached out to set a time to meet.

"This is Mortgage Mark. How can I be of service?"

"Uh, hello. Do you always answer the phone like that?"

"I sure do! Who do I have on the line?"

"Hi, Mark. My name is Jackie Thompson and Kelly Davis referred me to you this morning. A little while after that she called back and said it would be best if I called you to set up a meeting. This is my second home purchase with my husband, and I never even met our last loan officer, so I was a little surprised to hear that you wanted to meet in person to take the application."

"Sure Jackie, I can understand that and I appreciate your call. First, it's not absolutely required that we meet to take the application, but I know I can deliver a better experience to you if I take the most complete and thorough application possible up front. It's probably been a few years since you've been through this process and you can't believe how much information and documentation I'm going to need. How long has it been?"

"Oh, I'd say it's been about nine years or so. We bought our first home right before the crash, so it was probably a little fast and loose back then. I think I've got most of the stuff you'll need in one place. What types of documents do you need?"

"I'll e-mail you a list but first, let me ask you a few questions . . ." and with that, Mortgage Mark launched into his regular spiel of everything needed for the application. During the quick phone interview, he was careful to look for any areas that may need specific attention. By the time he was done, he'd added five things to the list he would send.

Without even looking at a bank statement or tax return, Mark had ascertained that Jackie's husband had been self-employed for quite some time; they'd recently sold their house and deposited the funds into their bank account; and they also owned one investment property.

Good thing I started this new method. This scenario is a bit more unique. What a nightmare it would be if I discovered this vital information after the first round of document gathering! And how frustrated would Jackie be if she'd have to ask for this information close to closing. But at least this is a good $400,000 loan—well worth the extra effort for these borrowers.

Mark ended the conversation by setting an appointment with Jackie for the next day. Since they were just under contract, time was of the essence. He impressed upon her the limited time they had to get through the loan process. Tyler had stressed that this was absolutely key, so Mark made it the foundation for his new Q&E method: all documents *must* be gathered within the first twenty-four hours in order to be successful.

Mark was excited and determined to make this a seamless experience for everyone involved. He was so excited, he almost forgot he still hadn't heard from his wife.

CHAPTER 25
BECOMING THE TWENTY PERCENT
43 DAYS

Mark was on cloud nine. His meeting with Jackie Thompson had gone extremely well, and she was already praising him for being so thorough and professional.

What an amazing change!

He had gone from doing just enough and feeling poorly about himself and his career to being praised before the approval had even come in! He'd even made a copy of everything she had provided on the spot, and they'd logged in to her online bank accounts to pull anything she didn't bring with her. By the time they'd finished, the only document missing was the insurance information for the investment property—but even that was in the works from the insurance company.

Mark escorted Jackie out of the office. To his surprise, she hugged him. Apparently he had properly impressed upon her that he was *the* mortgage professional for her family. Mark vowed to make sure this loan process went off without a hitch. He turned around to find both David and the receptionist's wide eyes. They'd been discussing something, but had stopped to witness Jackie's departure. David looked shocked.

"Looks like you had a good meeting?" David smirked.

"Yeah, it went very well, actually. My new business practices are starting to make a big difference." *Okay, I'm really going to say this.* "And as you already know from Linda, my files are looking much better. I'm really looking forward to the next forty days." With that, he turned on his heel, walked into his office and closed the door. It was arrogant, he knew, but he was feeling so good right now, he couldn't resist.

Why haven't I been doing this for the last few years? Sure, it's more time-intensive, but what a huge difference!

He doubted that this loan would ever be in jeopardy. He could practically bank the commission, not to mention the positive impact this would have with Kelly. She would look like a rock star to Jackie for referring her to someone that made a normally difficult and arduous process look and feel easy. Mark went to his office and began the process of uploading the documents into the LOS. As soon as he sat down, he realized how time-intensive the Q&E method really was.

He'd met with Jackie at 8:15. She left around 9:30. That was seventy-five minutes for the appointment, not to mention the thirty minutes he'd spent yesterday on the phone. Now he was scanning, which would take another ten minutes and probably another ten minutes to separate, name, and upload everything. He rounded his total time investment so far to a full two-and-a-half hours.

Dang! That's a long time and I haven't even started chasing conditions yet.

Mark was used to spending between thirty and forty-five minutes from taking an application to uploading minimal documentation. Plus, he rarely if ever scanned and sorted documents—he usually just let Linda figure it out. If this was going to be his new norm, Mark realized he would need an assistant fairly quickly. He was beginning to truly understand why some of the most successful originators in the country had built teams around themselves. *I can't wait to share this with Tyler.*

Once the documents had been uploaded and named, Mark moved the file to the next stage. It was hands-off from here on out. Mark shot a quick e-mail to Linda describing the scenario and everything that had been uploaded, specifically mentioning the missing insurance. This way she could get a quick rundown of the file and know why he'd collected what he collected and where things were at. *I can't wait to see Linda's reaction to this file!*

His phone buzzed—a text message from Jennifer. Mark eagerly unlocked the phone to read what she'd written. They'd talked off and on yesterday via text and the tone was still icy. Mark could never understand why, but this was Jennifer's preferred communication method when she was upset. She said it was because she wanted to keep her emotions in check, but it was incredibly time-consuming.

Time is threatening to eat me alive today.

This one was fairly simple: "We'll be back Sunday night from my parents. See you then."

Mark responded quickly and laid the phone down. Thankfully, they'd be back in a few days. Mark wanted so much to explain to Jennifer what steps he was taking to keep his word, and he wanted a chance to make it up to Jason. He knew it'd take time and action, but they'd left so suddenly, he hadn't been given a chance to do anything.

Mark heard a soft knock at the door and beckoned the knocker in. Stan held a colorful piece of paper in his hand.

"Here it is. My latest masterpiece!" Stan grinned, clearly impressed with himself.

Amused at Stan's enthusiasm, Mark took the paper and looked it over. It *did* look good, and it was exactly as he'd sketched it. Now, he just needed it to be bigger so he could put it on his desk.

"Man, this looks awesome, Stan. Another great job! I want this to be on my desk so I can see it every day and schedule things on the fly. Is it possible to blow this up like those calendars we get from the title companies?"

"Yeah, no problem. How many do you want?"

"Let's start with four, and if it ends up working out, I'll probably have you print another forty-eight. One for each week."

"Okay, sounds good, boss. I'll bring them by later."

Mark turned to his computer and scanned through his messages. He saw one from Tyler and immediately opened it.

"Hey, I need to change our meeting from tomorrow to today if at all possible. I need to meet someone tomorrow or we'll have to meet next week otherwise. Let me know and we'll go same time, same place today."

Mark immediately fired off an e-mail.

"That works. I'm going to eat ahead of time at the office. A new thing I'm doing. See you then."

Mark patted himself on the back for sticking to his plan with lunch. It would have been easy to just meet Tyler and buy something there, but it would have been a step backwards. *I don't need anything else to feel guilty about.*

Mark spent the next two hours setting appointments with the agents whose names he'd been provided with yesterday. The Consumer Referral Program and Q&E had catchy enough names that they intrigued the agents. It also helped that he was promising an increase to their business.

Yesterday, he'd set specific parameters for the type of agents he wanted to meet. According to Todd Duncan, approximately twenty percent of agents did about eighty percent of the business. That meant the market was flooded with low producing agents that would *never* lead to a meaningful increase in *either* of their businesses. Mark had previously been guilty of meeting with these low-producers because it allowed him a "pass" by feeling productive, simply because he was taking actions that were deemed to be good. *No more. That's not exactly efficient, is it?*

His alarm went off at 11:15 a.m.

CHAPTER 26
DEALING WITH MESSY CREDIT REPORTS
43 DAYS

Mark met Tyler at the same restaurant as before, but they opted to actually sit down at the coffee shop next door. With coffees in hand, they grabbed a booth away from the door, secluded from the drone of other day workers and stay-at-home moms enjoying the atmosphere. Mark wasn't sure what they were going to cover today. Tyler hadn't mentioned anything specifically.

After a tentative sip, Tyler winced and started the conversation "Damn, that's hot. Why do they have to make it that hot when you're going to sit here and try to drink it?" Tyler took a deep breath to funnel some cool air into his mouth and looked at Mark. "So, do you have any success stories? Were you able to implement what we talked about?"

Mark's slight smirk morphed into a broad smile. "Actually, yes and yes. I started by taking your advice to speak with agents to get referrals to other agents. I dropped the ball a bit by not actually getting a referral to another agent on the first round, but one of my top agents handed me a client. I encouraged her to have the client meet me in person so I could thoroughly implement what we talked about. So, we met today and it went really well . . . no, in fact, it went great! I was shocked. I actually came up with a name for the method that you described to me. I'm calling it the Quality and Efficiency Initiative. Q&E for short."

Tyler blew on his cup of scalding lava before responding. "Wow, that's terrific! You'll have to keep me updated on that file. You know, I hadn't even thought to give my method a name, but I like Q&E. It's fitting. Do you mind if I borrow that?"

"Of course not! It's your method."

"Okay, good deal." Tyler looked at Mark while taking another sip from his black lava. "You seem a little down. Everything all right?"

Mark rubbed his face and didn't respond right away. He could easily brush the question away and blame it on having a bad night of sleep. *Did it really matter to involve Tyler into my latest round of problems? Maybe I should try honesty as my policy for once. Especially if Tyler's taking time help me. I owe it to him to be honest.*

"Yeah, it's fine. After we met last time I got too wrapped up in working on this stuff and I didn't make it to my son's soccer game on time. Unfortunately, my track record for attending his games is terrible, so this was just in addition to the problems that I've had. I broke my kid's heart. I destroyed his trust in me. Jennifer is barely speaking to me and was so furious, she took Jason the next morning to go spend a few days with her folks. So, in addition to getting my work life on track, apparently I'm in just as much hot water at home."

Tyler nodded. "Oh, man. Been there, done that! It's so easy to get wrapped up in work that family and other important things often go by the wayside. I'd say there's no perfect method, but there are things you can do to get things back on track at home, even if that means your personal production needs to take a temporary backseat. I will say this though, any time I was honest with my borrowers, realtors, and other team members about how my family would always take precedence, I actually got a lot of support from them. After being assured their loan would not be affected, I think they respected my principles. Of course, there will be times when you need to work late or on the weekend, but that's the mortgage business. It's just the nature of the beast. No one is going to die if they don't get a callback immediately. But as you've experienced, you can cause serious damage to your family just from being late."

"Yeah, I agree. That makes sense. By sharing my priorities and commitments with my borrowers, I'll be able to set proper expectations with them and develop trust. It will go in line with my struggle to have integrity in all aspects of my life. It's just personal growing pains." Unintentionally, they sipped simultaneously.

Switching gears, Tyler asked, "So, you mentioned a new client. Tell me how that went?"

Mark spent ten minutes filling him in on his conversation with Kelly and how things had gone with the borrower. He ended by saying, "I'm not really sure what else you and I are going to talk about today. The methods I learned a few days ago are likely to solve a huge portion of my problems."

Tyler chuckled and took another sip of coffee. "Without a doubt, you're on the right track, but from the sounds of it, that was a relatively easy file and you were able to get the documents that you needed upfront from an accommodating borrower. What happens when you have a messy credit report, or the borrower physically can't locate necessary documents?"

"Yeah, you're right. There's all kinds of things that could cause my new method to blow up. Okay, sensei. What's my lesson?"

"Alright, grasshoppa. Tell me about what you do with the credit report."

"Well, I suppose it's pretty basic. Once I get to the part of the application concerning the credit report, I'll keep the borrower on the phone while I look for any issues like late payments. My primary concern is just the score since that will dictate what program and what rate they'll qualify for."

Tyler gave him a funny look, causing Mark to ask, "Alright, what's wrong with that?"

"Nothing wrong, it's just not enough. Yeah, the credit scores are going to drive a huge portion of the loan, but what if the borrower has late payments on student loans, vehicles, medical debt, or what-have-you? All those things can cause issues if you don't know how to handle them. Knowing the guidelines are very important. We're going to stick with credit, but let me ask: do you regularly review Fannie Mae or FHA guidelines?"

"No, I don't spend a whole lot of time studying the guides any more. Generally, our company will release a snippet if it's important, but unless I see a huge problem I've encountered before, I'm going off the AUS decision and credit report. Those go hand-in-hand, so I either get the Approve/Eligible or I don't."

Tyler shook his head. "Okay, we're coming back to that today, but it's just not enough. You need to *know* those guidelines *and* be able to quote them. That may seem like overkill, but not structuring a loan correctly is what usually kills the deal. A dead deal isn't necessarily due to the borrower's facts and circumstances. Back to the credit report, the other major thing you should do is confirm *all* derogatories and *all* successful lines with the borrower."

"What? That's crazy. Do you know how much time that will take?" *Now I understand why successful LO's have teams. Geez.*

"Will it take more time than trying to piece a file back together after it's crashed? Probably not. Plus, it only takes like five minutes. Generally what I do here is jot down some notes about the lines so the borrower can complete an LOE."

"Okay, okay." Mark wrote more notes again.

"Moving on from there, the final thing you should pay close attention to are the addresses at the bottom. They're rarely perfect, but it will allow you to spot something unusual and possibly inconsistent with what the borrower is telling you. I'm not saying they're intentionally trying to commit mortgage fraud, but they may have received poor guidance from someone in the past warning them about volunteering information. You might find business addresses or previously owned or currently owned addresses—all sorts of things you need to document *before* that file goes into underwriting. Otherwise, you're going to be trying to prove to your underwriter *after the fact* that those problems aren't a problem which will lead to more frustration. Any questions on the credit report? If not, we'll move back to the guidelines."

Mark shook his head no.

CHAPTER 27
READ THE GUIDELINES AND THE FINDINGS
43 DAYS

"So, going back to the guidelines. You *have* to, HAVE TO, start reading these, especially if you're encountering a scenario you haven't seen before. I can't tell you how many LO's don't even know where to find the guidelines on the Internet. Do you know how marketable that makes you when speaking with realtors and prospects? If you can position yourself as *the* expert, why wouldn't they get a loan from you? Product and price don't matter at that point because they trust that what you're telling them is solid information, and you won't have to deal with a broken file later. Does that make sense?"

"Yeah, it does. So what do you recommend?"

"After we meet today, I recommend that you read the entire handbook for Fannie Mae, FHA, and VA. It's going to take you a few hours, but it will be well worth it. Then, continue to refer to these *every time* you have a loan scenario that you don't one hundred percent feel certain about. Heck, even include a snippet of the guidelines for the processor and underwriter so they don't have to question why you did something."

"Hmm, that's a great point about including the snippet of the guidelines. That'll show them I've done my research and that it's valid."

"Absolutely. Now, I brought up the guidelines to bring up this point, which is crucial. You need to be *validating* the AUS findings with the borrower at the point of the application."

Mark sat silently, blinking at Tyler. "This is starting to be a little much. At what point am I doing so many things that I can't go out and get another loan?"

Tyler leaned back in his chair and folded his arms, abandoning the coffee that was almost too hot to drink. "It's a valid point. I believe you told me once that you're hitting somewhere around five units a month, is that right?"

"Yeah, I'd say that's the average. Every once in a while I'll hit more, but that's generally due to some refi business."

"Well, I developed this metric, and it's by no means a hard-and-fast rule, but at around five unit blocks you need to add a member to your team. So, you're actually about due for an assistant if you don't have one already."

Mark furrowed his brow. "I'm not sure I can afford an assistant right now. Jen and I have a little income left over each month, but this would put us in a tough spot—remember, I've got a baby on the way."

"I totally understand where you're coming from, Mark, I've been there and I know it's a tough decision. Perhaps you can get your company to partner with you on covering the cost, but it's *absolutely critical* that you get some help soon if you're going to really build your production. Think about it. Do you enjoy getting docs? Do you enjoy chasing down minor things? Wouldn't your time be better spent learning about products, meeting and educating realtors, and more importantly spending time with your family? An assistant will allow you to do that. And then you'll need another, and another. By the time you're hitting twenty units a month, there should be about four people on your team, including you. We'll get into the specifics of that later. Let's just get the foundation right first so you can take your game to that next level."

Mark stared into the distance, dreaming about such a future and taking another sip of coffee. Burning his tongue brought him back to his current reality.

"All right, sounds good. So, what the heck am I supposed to do with these AUS findings? I don't even remember the last time I actually completely read what they said."

"You're certainly not alone there. I'm one of the few people I know who does. What you need to remember is that your underwriter is underwriting to *these findings*, for the most part. So if the findings flag something that needs to be taken care of and it's not, you either have another condition, or you could easily have a suspense or a dead loan. The nice thing about the AUS findings is that they're generally grouped together and somewhat follow how the application is segmented."

Mark nodded for Tyler to continue.

"For example, the findings analyze the credit report and will tell you if there are accounts that need to be addressed. This is obviously crucial because it can take days or weeks for the credit bureaus and creditors to comply with a request. Moving on from there, the AUS will analyze assets and reserves. Depending on the number of financed properties it detects, the credit score, and the overall risk profile, the AUS will ask for differing amounts. If you have a first-time home buyer or someone who has limited cash, this could be a deal breaker right there. Plus, the findings are generally in easy-to-read sentences, so it's not like you're trying to decipher hieroglyphics. If the AUS asks for something, you verify the condition with the borrower, and then you ask for whatever documentation you need. Less than five percent of my files have had a problem when I've validated the findings with the borrower. If necessary, I'll also ask for additional documents from the borrower based on a review on my own."

"Wow, I never really paid much attention to the findings unless I got a Refer or Ineligible. No one ever trained me how to read them. Geez, after talking to you I feel like I'm lucky just to have made it this far." *Guess I should have taken some of those free classes always being offered.*

"Haha, I know the feeling. Honestly, you haven't probably been so much lucky as you've just been tenacious as hell. And you've paid for it. You told me yourself that you're feeling really burnt out and not enjoying this business like you used to."

"Is there anything else? My hand's getting sore and I'm not sure how much more information I can process this round."

"I'll share one final thing and then we'll call it quits. Now that we've talked about how important it is to know your guidelines and thoroughly review the credit report and findings with your borrower, we need to talk about supporting documents. We talked the other day about what needed to be gathered from the borrower up front, but there's plenty you can gather behind the scenes that's either preemptive or will save you in the event your borrower's scenario requires a little creativity."

Mark turned the page on his notepad, flicked his wrist a few times to shake the cramp, and mumbled, "Fire away."

"Without a doubt, bank statements are the biggest pain in the ass that you, your borrower, or your processor are going to face. If the AUS findings allow it and your guides support it, you can pull a verification of deposit. Do you know what that is?"

"Not really. I've heard the term thrown around a few times, but I don't know what's required and I don't know what it does."

"Regardless of whether you use bank statements or a VOD, you absolutely must lay eyes on the assets that will pay the down payment and closing costs. You should never submit a file to underwriting unless the funds to close are clearly documented. Otherwise, the file is dead on arrival. Now, speaking of VOD's, every program and guideline is a little different, but as long as your borrower's average balance has remained relatively consistent, you can pull a VOD so that you're not having to track down a million deposits. This can often replace the bank statements if the AUS findings allow for it. This is a huge time-saver, especially if you have a self-employed borrower. It can also save a deal because your borrower may not be able to satisfactorily explain where some deposits came from. But if the balance is within the threshold, you're fine."

"Well hell yes, I can see where this could be a *huge* help. I wonder if my processor even knows about this."

"I'm sure she does but again, not all programs allow them. Again, this is where it pays off to learn the guidelines. Until you know this inside and out, continue asking for bank statements just to be safe. You can always include or exclude anything you need from the file. Following in that thought, I know TRV's tend to cause last-minute struggles on a good deal of files. I recommend that you work with your team to get those ordered the moment you take the application and can verify the exact name that appears on the tax return. That way you can reorder if something happens. I'd also make sure you're pulling the W-2 transcripts so you have those in the file as well. These all cost a little bit of money, but they lead to a much better experience for both you and the borrower, and it makes you look like a true professional if you're not constantly going to them with problems or asking for more paperwork."

"So, in summary, I need to work with my processor to create a policy around what and when I'd like these things ordered as long as they're in line with what the AUS findings are telling us?"

"Yeah, you got it!"

"Whew! I'm ready to call it a day. Is it 5:00 yet?," Mark joked. He felt like he was taking Mortgage 101 again. "Well, I'd better get back to the office. I've got some more calls I'd like to make so I can keep feeding the pipe for this month."

"Sounds good. When we meet next week, we'll talk about some sales tactics and any problems you're seeing from your process."

CHAPTER 28
GAINING GROUND
40 DAYS

The next few days flew by in a blur for Mark. All he could think about was Jennifer and Jason coming home so he could work on mending his relationship with them. He'd been incredibly busy at work, which had helped.

After meeting with Tyler, Mark had scheduled a meeting with Linda to discuss what he was looking to do and how they could implement it. Luckily, she was familiar with VOD's and agreed to start ordering them when possible and agreed to be proactive about ordering TRVs and other services upfront as well. During the meeting, Mark even came up with an idea to start sending out an advanced DocuSign package so his borrowers could quickly e-sign the 4506T, the Borrower Authorization and Certification, and the Consent to do Business Electronically. Under current regulations, these three documents would allow the team to get started even quicker. As the meeting ended, Mark asked Linda to keep an eye out for an assistant. He had zero idea where to source someone like that, and he knew he'd need some help.

"Wow, Mark, you're looking for an assistant?"

"Yeah, I've been meeting with a mentor since going to that Todd Duncan conference. He recommends that I get one so I can take my business to the next level. I'm trying to get to twenty loans a month now."

Linda looked at him incredulously. "Isn't that like *quadruple* your production? How in the world are you going to get there?"

Mark smiled and shrugged his shoulders. "I honestly have no idea, but I know I want to be a top dog in the industry. I'm tired of doing five loans a month and not living the life I want to live. Plus, I'm tired of dealing with all the issues we've faced over the last few years. I'm tired of being complacent and mediocre. By following these new methods, I'm hoping to have cleaner files in order to do more business with less stress. By the way, what did you think of the file I sent in the other day?"

Linda laughed. "Honestly? I was shocked at how complete and clean it was. I just ordered my handful of services and sent it in just a bit ago. We'll probably get an answer fairly quickly, and we might be able to close this one *very* early if everything pans out. Did your mentor teach you how to put a file together like that?"

"As a matter of fact, he did. I'm grateful to him and anxious to see where it takes us."

"Well, keep up the good work. I'll put in the good word for you with David."

On that emotional high, Mark reached out to a few more of his referral partners and set up meetings with them in their respective offices to discuss his business plan and get more business. It was amazing how easy it was to set up these meetings when they were warm introductions.

What a concept!

On Friday, Mark hired a maid to come in and clean the house from top to bottom. He wouldn't normally justify an expense like this, but Lord knows he had been so focused on his business plan that he had totally neglected the house. Besides, he needed to suck up to Jennifer. He walked in the door and was stunned at how clean the house looked and felt. The maid had ingeniously bought a handful of cinnamon apple scented wall plugs to perfectly mask the slight lingering scent of Pine Sol. All he knew was that it was clean, fresh and bright. Now all he had to do was make sure Boomer didn't crap all over the place and ruin it.

On both Saturday and Sunday morning, Mark spent extra time getting specific and clear on his goals. Earlier in the week, Hal Elrod's podcast had featured someone who recommended having a goal of reviewing your other goals at least once a week to make sure you were staying on track. Mark's goals now included taking a trip once a quarter with Jennifer, sending Jason to soccer camps, providing the baby with top-notch early education, and improving himself constantly through reading books and maintaining physical activity.

On Sunday afternoon, Mark chose to take it easy and watched some football on TV. It was hard to focus on anything. This fight with Jennifer was uncomfortable and he didn't know what to expect. He'd throw himself at their mercy and show them how he'd been working on—and would continue to work on—keeping his word and putting them first.

At a little after 7:00 p.m., Mark's phone buzzed.

"Hey, in the driveway. Jason's asleep. Can you help?"

Mark jumped up and tossed the phone on the couch. On the way out, Mark hustled Boomer out the back door. The last thing he needed was Boomer to start barking or to trip him up with Jason in his arms. Jogging out to the driveway, he saw Jennifer staring at him through the windshield. There was no smile or scowl or finger gestures. From the look on her face, he couldn't tell if she'd forgiven him or if she was still upset. Hopefully, the clean house would win her over.

As carefully as possible, he grabbed the handle and pulled it toward him to disengage the lock. Thankfully, it opened without a sound and he slid the minivan door back slowly. Jason was slumped over in his car seat sound asleep. Mark marveled at how hard the kid slept. Jason regularly made it through bad thunderstorms without waking up. Mark hoped that would hold true now. He really needed to debrief with Jennifer and get back to square one so he could start the week fresh.

With expert precision, he unbuckled Jason's seatbelt and scooped his son out of the car, quickly laying his head over his shoulder and cradling his body against his chest. Sure enough, Jason barely stirred as Mark walked toward the house. Behind him, he heard Jennifer's door open and close gently. Mark took Jason straight to his room, laid him down and gingerly unlaced his little Nikes. Luck was on his side tonight. After tucking him in, Mark moved back into the hallway and closed the door behind him. He heard Jennifer in the kitchen getting something to drink.

As he approached her, Jennifer smirked. "I appreciate your peace offering with the house. It looks wonderful. I'll scratch through part of your name on my shit list."

Mark smiled and hugged Jennifer. She didn't reciprocate, but he knew the worst was over. They spent a few minutes catching up on what had happened over the last few days. Jennifer opened up some, but it would take more time for her attitude to thaw. Mark decided he would fill her in on his progress, starting with his commitment to improve his integrity, no matter how small.

"It may seem silly to you, Jen, but I've even committed to only eating the lunch I take with me to the office each day or not eating at all. I think it was the little things over time that got me on the path that I've been on."

"Yeah, I guess that makes sense. But how soon will it be before I see changes that really matter?"

"Very soon. I'm working on it every single day so you'll see it both in little and big things."

"Um hmm, we'll see."

Mark switched gears to new developments with his Miracle Morning. Her ears perked.

"I've actually started to enjoy meditation lately. It was nearly impossible at first, but I can't tell you how much it's helped me focus on tasks and even reach deep into my consciousness to figure out what's important to me."

She looked skeptical. "Huh, that is interesting. I've never seen you sit quietly. Ever. I think it would kinda be like watching a dog walking on its hind legs."

"Oh, ye of little faith!" Mark chuckled and clutched both of her hands and kissed them. She didn't pull back. He guided the conversation to a more serious note: work.

"So, moving on to work, things have both gotten better and haven't really changed much at all."

"What do you mean? Is what you're doing not working?" Jennifer tightened her grip and instinctively laid her other hand against her stomach, as if to shield the baby from more bad news.

Mark grimaced. "No, it's definitely working. I've already seen some great results, I'm just in the awkward transition phase. My old pipeline is closing out and moving forward on the new pipeline, I'll be implementing the new methods. I'm meeting again with Tyler later this week to talk about sales strategies and how to build my pipeline the right way. I've also had a few breakthroughs about how I want to pursue business so that it's both meaningful and profitable to me and my clients and partners. It's strange though. For as much grief as management gave me to improve, I don't feel like they're coming alongside me to help. Even when it looks like things are getting much better . . . " his voice trailed off for a second. *How could David NOT notice? He saw that email last week from Linda and Teri.*

He witnessed a client actually HUG me because she was so pleased with my service. He knows of my investment in Todd Duncan and that I'm working with a mentor. "I just don't know what to make of it, Jen. It feels like a "sink or swim" situation."

The explanation seemed to have successfully comforted Jennifer. After a few more minutes of talking, they moved upstairs to sleep, in the same bedroom no less.

CHAPTER 29
ESTABLISHING AN ABUNDANT LIFE
39 DAYS

During part of his Miracle Morning the next day, Mark journaled ways he could improve on his integrity not only with his family, but also in business. As he thought of example after example of how he'd taken the easy way out, the reason why he was struggling in most aspects of his life suddenly hit him like a bolt of lightning. He would over-promise and under-deliver in one area and blatantly ignore others. As much as he hated to admit it, Mark was surprised the fight with Jennifer hadn't occurred sooner.

Today's meditation was focused once again on his ultimate purpose. Even after weeks of searching, he still didn't feel like he had his one driving passion figured out.

Why is this *profession important to me achieving my goals? What is the most important thing to me?*

Mark racked his brain. Slowly, his mind drifted into visualization. Mark didn't fight the transition. This was complete freedom of thought, and he might have another breakthrough. From the depths of his mind, his bookshelf came into focus. Mark envisioned himself looking at each title, again, *Think and Grow Rich,* taking the fore-front. Andrew Carnegie's words poured out of the book: "Put all of your eggs in that one basket and watch that basket."

For many years, Mark had been torn as he perceived opportunity after opportunity passing him by in other industries. But all that did was act as a distraction. Now that he understood what heights could be achieved in the mortgage industry, he'd be crazy to devote his attention away from being the best mortgage banker he could possibly be. If he could channel his energy into increasing the depth of his relationships, this would in turn increase his quality referrals and boost his income.

And then it hit him. A few weeks ago he'd realized that public recognition was one of his chief motivations outside of providing for his family.

Land not only provides my family with a relatively stable and valuable asset, but also provides endless opportunities for development and sale. Additionally, land holders typically hold a certain prominence due to the rather public nature of the investment. My success in the mortgage business can be used to acquire vast acreage to change the financial trajectory of my family.

Ever since Mark was little, he marveled at families who owned hundreds of acres of land. When he passed by developments around town, he was green with envy.

Heck, maybe Jerry Jones should be my role model! He has a ridiculous amount of valuable land.

Mark journaled a few notes so he could reference them later, but felt clear and refreshed from this latest breakthrough. Finally, he felt like he had his master goal in mind—a goal that could be broken down into short- and long-term achievements.

As he cleaned up from his morning routine, the family calendar on the fridge caught his eye. Jason had a game this afternoon. Jennifer hadn't mentioned it to him. *Maybe it's a test?* It didn't matter. He planned to be there an hour early and work out of his car so he could jump out the moment Jason and Jennifer got there. Hopefully this would be the emotional deposit Mark needed to get back into Jason's heart.

When he got to work, Mark took a few moments and reviewed the previous business day to see if there were areas for improvement or practices he should start utilizing. A few minutes into his review, Mark recognized the need to implement this review every single day. There were clearly a few areas of "dead space" where Mark either couldn't account for his time or spent it on wasted activities that wouldn't increase his pipeline or further relationships with his referral partners or borrowers. This was a new best practice. In fact, not only would he review his previous day each morning while he was fresh, but he would also take time to review the day ahead on his new 7 Habits Calendar. His goals would constantly be reviewed and planned so he could stay on track.

Next, he reviewed his pipeline in the LOS to see where everything was at. The last of his problem files would be closing tomorrow, barring any unforeseen complications. His pipeline was low and he needed to do something about that. It wouldn't look very good for him to end his sixty-day probation period with only a few files in the system. It'd look like he already had one foot out the door. Getting his systems revamped was time-consuming. After the last few weeks, he only had four new loans. The upside was that he could almost guarantee that these loans would close *and* they'd close on time. That alone should generate new business.

From the recesses of Mark's mind came a shadow of a thought that would gnaw at him for weeks to come: *Why am I staying with my company? With all of this pressure to perform over sixty days, without any support, what will our relationship be like going forward?*

Mark quickly dismissed the idea, but it unsettled him. He had literally changed his life to stay with this company and get his act together. And the big boss *had* offered to reimburse him for the cost of the Todd Duncan conference if his business turned around.

But was it for the company, or was it for me? At this point, it was clearly for me.

After finishing a few notes on his 7 Habits Calendar, Mark tidied up his desk for an upcoming High Trust Interview with a fairly well-known and successful agent who he'd been referred to by Kelly Davis. Weeks ago, Mark wouldn't have dreamed of approaching this type of realtor. He simply didn't have a value proposition engaging enough to anyone of this caliber. Now, after a few referrals from existing relationships, he had a solid hour with Miles Wayne.

Mark reviewed his notepad of questions for the High Trust Interview. Glancing through a few options, Mark decided to stick with five and dive deep into those five for the full hour. Basically, the questions would prompt Miles to walk through what his purpose for being in real estate was, what his goals were, and how Mark and his new Q&E method could help Miles achieve his goals. The icing on the cake was the Consumer Referral Program. In fact, Mark had at least one lead to give to Miles in order to solidify the relationship and his commitment to helping Miles achieve his goals.

An hour later and Miles was vigorously shaking Mark's hand. "Wow, Mark, I can't remember the last time I actually enjoyed a conversation with a lender. And that includes the guy I'm currently using! I've been sending him deals for years. Nice enough guy but not only has he not reciprocated, but he's never even taken the time to ask me these types of questions. You already know in an hour what took me years to try to explain to my team—and my wife!"

Mark couldn't contain his smile. He was giddy. If Miles was being honest with him, this could be the game-changing relationship he'd been waiting for. On a personal note, he and Miles also appeared to see eye-to-eye on a lot of things. *This may even blossom into a genuine friendship.*

Listening to Miles had been inspiring. Mark was spellbound listening to the story behind Mile's crusade to achieve such lofty, ambitious real estate and income goals so he could donate as much money as possible to fight the disease that had claimed his first child. His baby girl, Beth, had only lived a few months. After months of grief, Miles started a foundation to help other families with children diagnosed with the same disease. This was not only therapeutic but was also the catalyst for Miles becoming one of the top realtors in Dallas *and* Texas. This was precisely the kind of person Mark wanted to spend as much time with as he could. In just the few short weeks he'd been doing the Miracle Morning, Tyler—and now potentially Miles—had significantly elevated his circle of influence.

Mark returned the vigorous handshake. "Miles, I truly appreciate your time, and I'm humbled to be speaking with someone of your caliber. I greatly admire what you do and want to immediately provide value to you and this new relationship, so here." Mark handed a slip of paper with a few notes to Miles. "This is a new client I've been working with who does not have a realtor. Regardless of what you can give me, I know you two will be a good fit and it will provide value to my client."

Miles was taken aback. "Uh . . . wow, Mark, I appreciate it. I've never—and I mean never—had a lender give me a referral, and at our first meeting no less!"

"Well, I want my customers to work with the best team possible and I know you'll take good care of them. I hope to send more referrals your way in the near future. Maybe we can grab a drink in a few weeks to catch up a bit more. A relationship outside of work."

"Hey, that sounds great. I'd love to."

They exchanged a few more words and Miles left. Mark was exhilarated, but he didn't want to ride this feeling too long. He had a lot of work to do.

———

"This is Mortgage Mark."

"Oh, hi Mark. Uh, this is Cindy, Cindy Fanning. Did Miles tell you that I would be calling?"

No, he did not, but this is a pleasant surprise!

"Hello, Cindy. Miles did mention that I may receive a call, but he likes to give his clients full control of that decision and conversation. How can I help you today?"

"Oh, okay. Well, I'm in the market for a house for my daughter. She'll be going off to college at SMU and I heard that it might, uh, might be a good investment to purchase a home in the area and have her and her girlfriends rent the property from me. Is that something you can help with?"

"Absolutely!" Mark tried to turn away from a gust of wind that hit him. "Can you hear me okay, Cindy?"

"Uh, yes I can. It sounds like you might be outside?"

"Yes, yes indeed. You actually caught me right before my son's soccer game. I've made a commitment to him that I'd be at every single one, but I'm thrilled to be receiving this call. Did Miles tell you how I like to do business?"

"He did mention that you'd prefer to meet in your office. I've never had to do that before. I'm not really sure it'd be worth it. Can't we just do everything online?"

"Well, we certainly could, but the lending world has gotten pretty complicated over the last few years. Have you purchased or refinanced recently?"

"Yes, actually. I refinanced my home with Quicken Loans at the start of the year and had a good experience. All from the comfort of my own home."

"Ah, I see. Yes, they're a huge company and do great work. How about this? Why don't I give you a call first thing in the morning and we can discuss if it makes sense to meet in person."

They finalized a time and hung up. From behind him, Mark heard, "Dad!"

CHAPTER 30
SUCCESS, ON AND OFF THE FIELD
28 DAYS

He whirled around just as Jason slammed into his knees full force. Luckily, Mark grabbed him before his ACLs paid the price. Over the last few weeks, Mark had been highly intentional about arriving to practices, games, home, and wherever he needed to be on time, or even early. It was often inconvenient, but keeping his word time and again had made large deposits into his emotional bank account with Jason. This was also yielding huge dividends with Jennifer, who had been very impressed with Mark's one-hundred-and-eighty-degree change.

"Alright son, get out there and score a goal for Papa Bear!" Mark set Jason on the ground and gently pushed his son toward the field. Jason skipped to the little ring of players circling the coach at midfield.

"It's good to see you here, Papa Bear. It means a lot. To all three of us." Jennifer cradled the slight bump from Baby Stiles.

"I wouldn't miss it for the world."

"What time is your meeting with Tyler tonight?"

"We're supposed to meet at 8:30 at our usual spot. I really didn't want to meet this late, but he's taking a vacation and there's a lot going on during this final stretch."

"It's okay. You've made every effort to put me and Jason first lately. I know you wouldn't do it unless you needed to." Jennifer squeezed Mark's hand and tiptoed her fingers to his ear. "Maybe if you're not gone too long . . ."

They watched the rest of Jason's game hand-in-hand.

CHAPTER 31
SECOND THOUGHTS
28 DAYS

"The first rule of Q&E is . . ." Tyler trailed off.

"You do not sacrifice Q&E?" Mark offered.

"Exactly! So, how's it been going?"

"You know, it's been going very well. A few times I've been tempted to cut corners, but then I remember how stress-free it's been over the last few weeks. Sure, every file has a few concerns, but nothing near what I was dealing with before. The thought of *not* doing Q&E stresses me out."

"Quick, what are the steps?"

"Completely fill out the 1003, starting with two years' residency, two years' job history with all jobs accounted for, a full understanding of how income is calculated with a detailed description of where the closing funds are coming from, followed up with a thorough review of the credit report analyzing each trade line, and finally validating the AUS findings with the information I've received. If I can do it in person with documentation in hand, I get bonus points. Do not pass go. Do not collect two hundred dollars."

"Hot damn!" Tyler slapped the table with his palm. "You'd think you were a good originator or somethin'."

"Ha ha. Very funny. I am a good originator. At least now anyway."

"So, what else is new?"

"Well, I met with Miles Wayne the other day and it looks like I've got that relationship in the bag."

"Terrific. Nice job! Miles does good work. That's a great relationship. I better watch my back. You'll be gunning for me next. Vader versus Obi Wan."

"Yeah, right. I'm hopeful, but I'm not going to put all my eggs in that basket just in case. I'll spread the wealth a little while longer and see which relationships work best. I've forged a ton of relationships since Sales Mastery, and I'm sitting in a good spot right now with regard to referrals and active files. Especially considering that the slower time of year is coming up."

"Any word from the boss man?"

"Very little, actually. Although they've offered little support I think they've realized that I took them seriously and it looks like I've done enough to keep my spot on the roster."

"That's good news. That must be a huge relief."

"Yeah, it is. In a way. But I'm having second thoughts about staying with them."

"Oh? Why is that?"

"I'm not feelin' the love. I've made a significant turnaround in a very short period of time and they've practically ignored me. I wasn't expecting a medal or anything, but you would think they'd take more of an interest in the changes I've made. Hell, they didn't even ask me to share with the other guys that were struggling! You'd think they'd care more about trying to get everyone back on track. I don't know . . . it seems like a shape-up or ship-out mentality. I asked if they'd be willing to support the Todd Duncan material and I was promptly told that they follow one, and only one, sales training method. I'm on my own if I want to pursue Duncan and the Miracle Morning. No additional support—even though my regional manager offered to reimburse me for the conference if I turned things around."

"Hmm, I see. How much thought have you put into quitting?"

"Quite a bit." Mark paused to gather the courage to ask what he'd been thinking about for days. "I've been thinking about applying to join your team."

A knowingly look flashed across Tyler's face. "So you think you're good enough to join the dream team, huh? A few days with Todd Duncan and a few weeks with Hal Elrod and suddenly you're a hot commodity?"

"Well, yeah, I think so. You've been instrumental to the changes I've made and I think I could boost the production of the team."

"Hell, I'm just givin' you a hard time, Mark. I'd love to have you join me. In fact, I was waiting for a good opportunity to sweep in and offer you a job. I've already cleared it with my regional manager and corporate. I'm impressed with how quickly you picked up the Sales Mastery training and the changes you've made from doing the Miracle Morning. You don't come across someone like that every day, and you're practically already doing business the Tyler Way. It's a no-brainer."

Mark smiled, "Hmm, well now that I'm a hot commodity, *show me the money!*"

CHAPTER 32
INFINITE POSSIBILITY
27 DAYS

"David, I quit."

Mark had rehearsed and envisioned this moment for several days, but no one can ever really prepare themselves for walking into their boss's office and dropping the Q-bomb.

David looked perplexed. "Mark, I don't understand. You've still got a few weeks left and we haven't put any additional pressure on you. We thought you were making good changes. I'm a bit shocked."

"I'm honestly surprised to hear you give me that feedback, David. I've made huge strides in my originations and file quality yet it's been complete silence from you and Paul. I appreciate the opportunity you guys gave me instead of just firing me a few weeks ago, but I've thought about this a lot over the past month. I don't think we're a good fit anymore."

"Is this because we didn't pay for that Duncan conference? I'm sure we could work something out."

"No, it's not about the money, David. It's about the support. Or lack of support, I should say. It's been made abundantly clear to me over the last month that we're not a good fit. There's another company that already supports my new way of doing business. In fact, it's practically responsible for my new lease on life. Again, I appreciate the opportunity that I've had here, but this is my last day."

Mark promptly stood up, shook hands with a stone-faced David Parsons, and walked out of his branch manager's office for the last time. He didn't want to make a big deal about his departure, but he did want to let a few people know he was leaving. He didn't give any details, just that he had a great opportunity with a longtime friend.

Although he initially thought leaving would be bittersweet, it was genuinely one of Mark's happiest moments of the year. He was walking away from old habits that had pulled him down and kept him from living a life on his terms, a life he was proud of and excited to live. Ahead lay infinite possibility. Not only for his family, but for the people he'd help along the way.

Beyond that office lay a brave new world, and Mark Stiles was eager to conquer it.

CHAPTER 33
ONE YEAR LATER

"I can't believe this is actually happening."

Nervously rubbing the stubble on his face, Mark grinned at Tyler. They were backstage at the annual Todd Duncan Sales Mastery conference as honored guest speakers. In minutes, they'd be speaking to attendees about their approach to business and their execution of Todd's strategies—particularly the High Trust Interview and their own Consumer Referral Program.

"I know. This is incredible, isn't it?" Pacing backstage, Tyler was smiling ear-to-ear. In front of the curtains, Todd rallied the crowd. A backstage assistant pointed to her wrist and gestured to Mark and Tyler that they'd go on in two minutes.

Two minutes! God, I hope I don't fall down walking across the stage.

Mark broke into a small sweat as Todd began their introduction.

"Okay, guys. First up today are two guys from a mortgage company that I've really enjoyed getting to know over the last few years. It wasn't very long ago that Steven Avery, the CEO of HomeSource Mortgage, made a commitment to send up to twenty-five attendees per year to Sales Mastery. Twenty-five attendees per year! Can you imagine the impact to your organization with a sales force that was determined and had a plan in place? Steven, are you in the crowd today?"

There was a brief pause as Todd scanned the crowd. After a few moments he located Steven, waved, and plowed ahead with his introduction.

"Great, I knew you'd be here, Steven. Everyone, think about how amazing it is that the CEO of a fast-growing, independent mortgage bank is sitting in the crowd absorbing and learning this material himself. How encouraging if you're an LO or a regional manager to know that your leader takes *your* success seriously and is equipping himself and his company to support *you* in *your* sales and career goals. Everyone, can we just give a round of applause to Steven? In the twenty-plus years that I've been doing this, I've never seen this kind of commitment from a CEO of a mortgage company."

Mark didn't know Steven extremely well, but in the short time he had gotten to know him, he knew Steven would be blushing profusely, humbled by this public attention. The crowd applauded in full force. After a few moments, Todd quieted them.

"Sorry to put you in the spotlight like that Steven, but I think it's fantastic what you and your company are doing right now. Okay, group, as I mentioned, we've got two guys from HomeSource Mortgage today. Tyler Halpurn has been a longtime attendee of Sales Mastery and credits a large amount of his success to executing the High Trust Interview, as well as his personally developed, and Home-Source-supported, Consumer Referral Program. A few years ago Tyler was heavily influenced by another speaker, Donielle Shelton, who had developed her own Consumer Referral Program."

A number of attendees nodded their heads. Todd held up two fingers.

"The second speaker is a huge turnaround story who was introduced to me and Sales Mastery through Tyler just last year. On the brink of losing his job and totally burnt out, Mark Stiles attended Sales Mastery last year. It completely changed his life *and* his way of doing business."

More attendees nodded. Some clapped.

"I'll let them tell their stories, but they are absolutely *killing it* this year at HomeSource Mortgage. These two guys combined are on track to close eighty million dollars in funded loan volume. Give it up for Mark and Tyler!"

Mark and Tyler exchanged nervous looks backstage and walked toward the curtain. The time attendant held it open, and Mark squinted as the stage lights blinded him. His eyes adjusted as he made his way to Todd and the two seats awaiting them. Upon approach, Todd shook their hands and energetically patted each man on the back. Mark and Tyler stood side-by-side. Todd whispered, "Take a deep breath . . . you guys are gonna do fine. Just relax and enjoy the spotlight." The crowd was gracious, offering a huge welcome, and Mark saw Steven stand up from the crowd to encourage his top Dallas producers. A large contingent of HomeSource Mortgage LO's stood with him, wearing their signature black shirts with the red roof logo.

As the crowd noise died, Mark and Tyler took their seats.

Don't worry. You're ready for this.

They'd planned their speaking order on the flight to California. Since Tyler had been a disciple of Todd Duncan the longest, he would go first and relate how he'd made the most of Todd's conferences. He'd then explain his relationship with Mark, then Mark would wrap up with his story.

Easy peasy, lemon squeezy.

Though Tyler would likely disagree, Mark marveled at how dynamic a speaker his boss and mentor was. The audience was fully engaged, frantically writing down as much information as they could. *I remember doing that exact same thing last year.* Tyler even managed to pepper his speech with a few chuckle-garnering jokes. Even though it had been fifteen minutes, it felt like no time at all before Mark heard himself being introduced by way of their recent journey together.

"I hope you guys enjoyed my story, and I really hope that you'll be the group that goes home and makes a difference in your offices, your careers, your life, and most importantly, your communities. It's my honor to introduce you to my friend, Mark Stiles!"

Thunderous cheers crashed onto the stage with a few whistles thrown in. The fired-up crowd wanted more. They waited in eager anticipation for Mark to blow them out of the water. As Tyler and Mark passed each other, they exchanged a low five and Mark took a deep breath.

"First off, let me tell you how *extremely* nervous I am right now."

The crowd laughed. Mark tried to control his breathing. If he wasn't careful, it would carry into his voice and he'd sound like an idiot. He knew he shouldn't be scared. He'd rehearsed his speech hundreds of time—first in front of Jen and Jason and then to in-creasingly larger crowds. Mark knew such practice was crucial or he'd freeze onstage.

"Well, let me tell you, it's been a crazy twelve months. About a year ago, I was in one of the worst spots I've ever been in my mort-gage career. I was feeling frustrated and burnt out. I wasn't enjoying originating any longer. And to make matters worse, my clients and team were suffering because I was dropping the ball badly on them. By sheer coincidence, I ran into my old buddy, Tyler at yet *another* networking event. You know, those frantic affairs that you attend with the intention of rubbing elbows with all the right people . . ." The masses nodded in unison so he let that thought linger before continuing. "Yep . . . I hadn't realized yet that the networking scene just wasn't working for me."

Mark panned the crowd, seeing all the knowing smiles. Obvi-ously, they'd suffered similar brain damage. Mark felt more confident now. *Mortgage misery loves company!*

He turned and pointed at Tyler. "This poor guy unwittingly and unofficially took me on as a mentee that night and the first thing he told me was, 'You've got to attend this Todd Duncan conference.' I couldn't think of anything I wanted to do less! Not only was it going to cost me money and time that I didn't have, but it was also self-improvement, which I had developed a strong loathing to. On top of that, I was facing termination at my company because of the sloppy practices I'd settled into."

Mark paused, allowing space for the crowd to consider their own likely irregular routes toward Sales Mastery.

"So, with my back against the wall, a skeptical attitude and no other hope in sight, I attended this same event last year. At that same time, Tyler convinced me to read this book called *The Miracle Morning*. Anyone in here read that book yet? Are you having Miracle Mornings?"

Quite a few people raised their hands. A few whistlers piped up.

"Hell, yeah! What a life-changing ritual! Believe me, I spent many years poo-pooing self-improvement books, hating all of that motivational crap . . . until I, myself, hit rock bottom. It's a very different perspective when it's YOU at the bottom of the barrel. Now I can't imagine functioning each day without my SAVERS routine and having a clear vision in mind thanks to Todd and his homework."

The crowd was receptive and Mark continued for another ten minutes, recounting the steps he'd taken, the ah-ha moments he'd had, and the methods he'd used to change his life. He talked about the difficult but important decision to leave his old company, which didn't support his newfound ideology and routines. He talked about what a difference it had made to join a company that embraced both the Miracle Morning and Todd Duncan.

"Folks, I'm telling you right now, you absolutely *must* have an accountability partner when you leave this event. You must make sure you're being supported in your efforts. There's nothing worse than hitting roadblock after roadblock when you have a solid execution plan but no help in driving it home."

When Mark finally concluded, both he and Tyler met at center stage. They took an actors bow to a standing ovation. Wave after wave of accolades rolled over Mark. And damn, it felt good!

What an amazing opportunity! I can't believe I just did that when I was sitting in that same crowd last year with zero direction.

Mark and Tyler headed backstage as Todd Duncan took the podium to prep the audience for the next speaker.

"Wow, wasn't that amazing, group? Another big thank you to Mark and Tyler and HomeSource Mortgage. Keep an eye on those guys. We may just have them up here again next year!"

A few minutes later, Mark answered his phone.

"So, how did your speech go, hon?"

They'd talked about Jennifer tagging along for the conference, but with Kate only a few months old, it would have been a logistical nightmare.

"Jen, you just wouldn't believe it! I was nervous leading up to it, but I got comfortable a few minutes in. What a rush!"

"That's wonderful. I'm so proud of you, babe! I can't believe all you've accomplished and what the last year has brought to you . . . and to our family."

"Thanks, sweetie. Listen, I've got to go talk to a few folks and then I'll give you a call later when we've settled in."

"Okay, sounds good. Love you."

EPILOGUE

On the flight home, Mark once again stared out the window. The plane was somewhere over Arizona, but his thoughts were on Dallas roughly a year ago. The transition from his old company to HomeSource Mortgage had been relatively smooth, and he'd been able to transfer most of his clients over too. Within two months he was producing more than he'd ever been able to thanks to the team approach Tyler employed at his branch, along with the newly coined Quality and Efficiency Initiative. Every file, every time, no exceptions. As Mark began to hit new levels of success, his circle of influence widened substantially. He was able to more easily meet with top agents who had heard of the quality of his work and were actually contacting him to discuss his practices and why *they* should be doing business with *him*.

The home office support for the team was absolutely crucial as well. Industry changes were happening on a weekly basis so he constantly received communication about new program changes, Help Desk Loan Scenario opportunities, and a myriad of tools that were at his disposal to reach and serve even more clients.

With less focus being spent on simply getting a file closed, Mark had been able to hone his focus and strategy and truly employ the Jerry Maguire philosophy of fewer clients and more attention. He was producing an increasing amount of units every month, but it was at his discretion, and he was able to work with clients on his terms. Plus, the deep dive approach was paying dividends as he developed truly lasting relationships with his borrowers that resulted in friendships, new introductions, and even business opportunities.

The big change came when Kate was born. They'd been blessed with a healthy pregnancy, and Mark's heart melted when he held his baby girl for the first time. Even Jason had adapted well. Jennifer and Mark had spent months reviewing their options and ultimately decided to move into Dallas's Lakewood neighborhood for better schools, better location, and better opportunities. And it was all possible thanks to the continued success he'd experienced through origination and the support he got from the home office and his team.

And to think I almost skipped that networking event!

It made Mark uncomfortable to even think about how differently things would have been. He honestly didn't know what his future life looked like, but he knew it couldn't possibly be better than where he was now. With all the good that had been happening in Mark's life, he always remembered one idea from J.J. Watt of the Houston Texans: "Success isn't owned, it's leased, and the rent is due every day." Every week, he and Tyler discussed ways to improve their business and work on more opportunities to increase their influence and success. No matter what, Mark refused to slip back into the habits of his old ways.

I need to get a little sleep before I land. I'm sure I'll be on daddy duty tonight to give Jen a rest.

Ever-so-contently, Mark reclined his seat so he could sleep and leaned against the window. It didn't take long to slip from consciousness.

Success is hard work, and you've got to work hard to pay the rent.

AFTERWORD

First, I hope you enjoyed this book. It follows the experience I've had both as Tyler and as Mark. Like many other originators, I suffered from a lack of inspiration and trying to figure out how to be successful when you have a million different things you can focus on or be distracted by. Above all, I love to teach, which is the underlying current of this book.

Before you can be successful in any endeavor, you have to figure out your *why*. If you don't know what your *why* is, you will constantly struggle. I know this from personal experience. No matter where you're at or what you're doing, you must take time each day, preferably in the morning with a Miracle Morning, and discover your purpose. Once you've discovered it, you must constantly revisit it to make sure you are taking actions daily to fulfill that purpose and achieve your goals. If you don't do this step first, everything else is wasted.

The second step is consistency, and it's what most salespeople lack. Whether they're riding the emotional highs and lows of a sale or lack thereof, a loan officer must remain focused at all times and not allow a setback to derail them from the daily tasks they must execute in order to be successful. Realtors don't just call themselves. Borrowers don't just magically materialize in front of you. Whether it's a time to call a set number of contacts, a networking function, or a daily pipeline review, you must do it. Every. Single. Day.

On a more technical note, the techniques described in this book were coined by the Executive Management team of Georgetown Mortgage in an effort to fix the problems we were experiencing in the manufacturing process of a loan. We follow a retail branch model, and the quality of files we were receiving by many of our originators were not high quality, professionally generated loan files. But the problem was not isolated to the sales team. We, being operations and management, didn't have the discipline to kick a file back until it was actually ready to be reviewed. Files would be turned in by originators, even top originators, that didn't have Approve/Eligible findings from DU, that wouldn't have a complete employment history, or that didn't show enough funds to close. The list could go on. This means that our production team (processors and underwriters) were working on files that may or may not close and files that needed ridiculous amounts of attention. Conditions could number in the twenties and thirties!

Finally, we said enough is enough and got serious about fixing the problem. Our solution was the Quality and Efficiency Initiative. At its core, it's Mortgage 101. Nothing in the Q&E Initiative is groundbreaking or difficult to do, but it does require discipline on the part of the originator and the ability to push back on borrowers and referral partners who do not understand how crucial it is to have a full file up front. Beyond the core, we had one branch that used these techniques. Every. Single. Time.

And guess what? That branch's loans close on time (actually weeks early, usually), with little stress on our corporate system, and the branch was receiving a massive amount of referrals from realtors who *had to* do business with that team. Imagine that! Additionally, this was a high volume branch with a high volume producer, which proves that great work can be performed, even with higher volumes.

So, whether you're new to the industry or just looking to reset your origination strategy, I suggest these steps:

1. Take a full and complete 1003 application. No exceptions. Outside of stocks, cars, etc., every single field should have information in it. This includes the following on every single file, no exceptions:

   a. Two-year residency history
   b. Two-year employment history with no gaps
   c. Sufficient funds to close accounted for, including gifts
   d. Credit information populated
   e. Real estate owned section complete
   f. Complete
   g. Every
   h. Single
   i. Field

2. A thorough review of the credit report. This isn't just looking to make sure that the scores are high enough to qualify for the loan program you've discussed with your borrower. This includes a thorough review of all open and derogatory tradelines. The more information you have up front, the fewer questions you'll have to answer later—questions that can take valuable time. It may even be erroneous accounts that throw off the borrower's DTI. I pulled a credit report one time where the daughter's report included both her accounts and her mother's liabilities that she wasn't even obligated to. Somehow, the credit bureaus had merged the reports and it took weeks to unravel that mess. Luckily, it was caught at the point of application and we were able to keep the file moving.

3. A thorough, line-by-line review of the AUS findings. This may sound crazy and completely outside the scope of being a loan officer, but all bets are off nowadays. The AUS findings are generally what the underwriters are underwriting to. There are all kinds of AUS conditions that can be listed that may save or kill your deal at the point of application. Can you use a VOD to remove questions about frequent deposits and withdrawals? Do you need more than two months of reserves? Is only one year of tax returns requested? All of these things can either mean more or less documentation from your borrower up front and can lead to a smoother—or more hectic—experience.

4. Have all documentation in advance. I mean *all* documentation. This may sound difficult or ridiculous, but the point isn't just to get the loan done. That's 2009 thinking. You want to get the loan done in a way that enhances your relationship with your clients and referral partners, not in a way that makes them second-guess why they got a mortgage from you to begin with. When you ask for everything up front, it looks *way* better than having to ask for another bank statement or tax return because you only got one instead of two, or another pay stub because you didn't get a full thirty days. The days of a one-touch file still exist. Since most programs are fairly vanilla nowadays, there's little guesswork as to what an underwriter is going to ask for. Side note: don't guess if the underwriter is going to accept the file or not. If you have doubts that your file fully explains your borrower's income or assets, I can guarantee you that your underwriter isn't going to accept it. Do yourself and your client a favor and do it right up front.

    a.   Basic Documentation:

        i.   Driver's license

        ii.   Social Security Card (FHA loans)

        iii. Thirty days most recent pay stubs

        iv. Two months of consecutive bank statements with all pages, even if blank, to support down payment and reserve requirements (more may be needed)

        v.   Two years most recent tax returns with all schedules

        vi. Two years most recent W-2s

        vii. Two years most recent 1099s (if applicable)

        viii. Current year P&L (self-employed)

        ix. VA specific requirements (DD-214, etc.)

5. Meet them in person to do all of this. "But wait, Millennials don't want to see me. They just want to sit at their houses in their pajamas and shop as many lenders as possible before settling to do business with one of them." While I won't discount the fact that many Millennials will want to do business almost entirely electronically or over the phone, the more emphasis you place on this being a personal and important relationship, the higher likelihood you'll have that they'll both meet you in person to conduct the application *and* choose you as their mortgage professional. Millennials are not *that* much different from their parents. They still want to rely on someone's advice when purchasing or refinancing a home because the general public simply doesn't understand the ins and outs of what it takes to get a loan and the implications that the loan will have on their finances. When you have a borrower meet you face-to-face in your office, or even at a location that works best for them, you're able to review their documents in real time and discover possible issues you'll have to revisit later such as business

losses, large deposits in bank accounts, rental properties on tax returns, issues on credit reports, etc. The list could be quite long. You're also building a personal relationship with that borrower which gives you a greater chance of success at securing the transaction and asking for referrals. A successful mortgage relationship can be highly profitable to you and your referral partners if you treat it right.

6. Set the right expectations up front. Do you know how easy that is to do and yet is rarely done? Setting the right expectations from the get-go will allow you to control your borrower's anxiety during a stressful period of time. It will also allow you to look like a rock star when everything flows smoothly because of your use of Q&E.

Originating and funding a loan is a lot like manufacturing a product. Just like in manufacturing, there can be glitches in the system or delays. Your organization likely publishes turn times (or it should). If you tell your borrower that it will only take two days to get an underwriting decision when you know full well they're four or five days behind, you immediately introduce stress into your relationship with the borrower. You'll have to go back to them again and again, usually with the client calling you, and say "I don't know why it hasn't happened yet, but I know it's getting close." When this happens enough times, you completely lose the borrower's confidence, and your chances of repeat business or referrals quickly evaporates.

Take control of the conversation and always tell the truth. If you have bad news, come with a solution if at all possible. Again, this is a relationship business, not a transaction business. You will find success much quicker when you fully embrace that concept. It all goes back to integrity.

Finally, there's culture. That's quite the buzzword in the wake of the Great Recession and massive regulatory overhaul. Now that mortgage companies essentially offer the same products and services, they are forced to differentiate themselves by their culture. Ultimately, you'll need to find the right organization that's in line with your values and how you like to do business.

One important aspect of culture is support. You need to find a mortgage company that will support how you like to do business and will assist you in achieving your goals. At Georgetown Mortgage, we've adopted three important concepts: Todd Duncan's teachings, Gary Keller's *The ONE Thing*, and Hal Elrod's *Miracle Morning*.

Todd Duncan's Teachings

There are many important things to learn from Todd Duncan, but arguably one of Todd's best works is *High Trust Selling*. *High Trust Selling* provides a loan officer with an important foundation for establishing trust with borrowers and referral partners and creating a lasting sales business. You simply cannot succeed if you treat all of your loans as one-time transactions. You will quickly earn a bad name for yourself and no one will want to do business with you. Word travels fast in real estate offices.

In addition to Todd's written works, we sponsor up to twenty-five loan officers a year to attend Todd's Sales Mastery and Sales Academy events. These two events are crucial to attend if you'd like to take your life and business to the next level. I've provided a brief glimpse of the events in this book, but you must experience them to fully understand what they offer and the impact that they will have on your life and career.

When an organization backs a specific technique, it allows you to seek support if you're struggling with execution. Georgetown Mortgage fully supports Todd's techniques and offers a variety of outlets to find support including calls, office visits, and role playing.

Gary Keller's *The ONE Thing*

If you haven't read *The ONE Thing* yet, you really need to look into it. The book provides straightforward steps to focus on the one thing that you need to do *right now* in order to achieve your goals. That ONE Thing could be reading this book. It may be doubling down on your database so that you have maximum influence over your past borrowers. It may be setting appointments with the realtors that you've been too timid to approach. You get the idea. If you aren't focusing on one thing at a time, you're bound to get priority dilution. That's a huge issue I struggled with during my originating career. *The ONE Thing* helped me to focus and figure out what step I could take to make the dominoes fall down in my favor.

Hal Elrod's *Miracle Morning*

Outside of a handful of events in my life, *The Miracle Morning* has been one of the most impactful. Interestingly enough, I experienced my first Todd Duncan Sales Mastery event and the guest speaker was Hal Elrod. In the same weekend, I had my professional career ignited by Todd Duncan and his guest speakers, and I had my life turned upside down by Hal Elrod's motivational speech and introduction of the Miracle Morning. At the time I attended the event, I was coming off my best origination month ever, but I felt like my life was completely out of control. I was dealing with quality issues in my files, I was in the worst shape of my life, and I was feeling disillusioned with originating because I was chasing that next commission. In short, I was having a hard time dragging myself out of bed to face the world. *The Miracle Morning* changed all that.

I started getting up at 5:00 a.m. each morning to figure out what my purpose was. I started meditating and journaling. I started to envision a life where I was fully satisfied with my work and providing an outstanding life for me and my wife. In just a few short weeks, I uncovered my driving passion that enabled me to enjoy my work again. I discovered how I wanted to conduct my business and make a difference in the lives of the people I worked with. I began expanding my circle of influence and being highly intentional about each minute I spent in the day. You get the idea, but it was a game changer for me, and it's been a game changer for everyone I've introduced the book to. Without a doubt, if you're looking to change your life, you need to start with Hal's book first. This is especially important if you're considering a career change into the mortgage industry or if you're looking to change companies.

I appreciate you taking the time to read this book. I hope that it will provide you with a reset button if you're struggling or a roadmap if you're just now getting into the business.

ABOUT THE AUTHOR

Michael Jones is a licensed loan officer and a resident of the great city of Austin, TX. After graduating with a B.A. in Accounting and a Masters of Taxation from Baylor University, Michael joined PricewaterhouseCoopers, LLP, in Dallas, TX, and became a licensed Certified Public Accountant. After spending a few years with PwC, Michael entered the mortgage industry and found success working with self-employed individuals and first-time homebuyers.

Michael is married to his high school sweetheart, Racheal, and is raising Samson and Judge (Great Danes), Roxy (mutt), and Calamity "Callie" Jones (a quarter horse).

To contact Michael about this book or to receive free additional content, email michael@resetnovel.com.

Made in the USA
San Bernardino, CA
27 May 2017